Volume 1

MINNESOTA MONOGRAPHS IN THE HUMANITIES

Gerhard H. Weiss, editor

PROSE STYLES

Five Primary Types

by

HUNTINGTON BROWN

The University of Minnesota Press, Minneapolis

PREFACE

M Y SUBJECT is a phase of the art of reading and my work an excursion into this art rather than a writer's manual. I think it well to make the point clear, from a suspicion that in the United States today any book published under a title containing the word "prose" is likely to be taken on sight for a handbook of composition for the college freshman. That the word should have become thus cribbed and confined is unfortunate. I can only hope that there are still readers to whom "prose" means something more interesting than what freshmen learn to put on paper in their weekly themes, and that some of these readers may find the present inquiry deserving of attention.

My point of departure is the question how to distinguish those features of a prose text that answer to the timeless function of its type from features accountable to fashion or the individuality of the writer. Accordingly I undertake to define within brief compass five types of style in prose that I conceive to be primary. Whatever may be thought of my account of them, I need hardly apologize for the direction of my effort.

I believe that I have raised some interesting questions, drawn some useful distinctions, and pointed under more than one head to striking generic similarities of style between writings as different in other respects as, for example, the Sermon on the Mount and Lamb's "Dissertation upon Roast Pig," or the sports columns of this morning's newspaper and *Beowulf*, or Aristotle expounding logic and the

5573

Gettysburg Address. At the time I completed my sixth chapter — on the indenture style — I had not been able to discover any earlier study of the kind I there undertook, and my whole manuscript was in print before a friend called my attention to Professor David Mellinkoff's *The Language of the Law* (Boston and Toronto: Little, Brown, 1963). This admirable volume, over five hundred pages in length, treats the evolution of this style in England and America very fully, in a lively spirit, and with a keen literary sense and a professional lawyer's knowledge. It would have afforded me invaluable help had I known of it; but I can now claim for my chapter, along with the convenience of its brevity, the high virtue of being confirmed in many of its observations by this writer's work. I can also claim to have glanced into one or two interesting matters that he, writing with more practical ends in view than mine, had no need and took no occasion to do, notably certain of the more distant sources of the style, and its influence in nonlegal literature.

I have tried to acknowledge my debts in full, and if I have anywhere failed to do so, I can only hope to be forgiven. I ask for charity also in case I seem anywhere to be merely laboring the obvious, for in a work of this kind it is not easy to avoid frequent reference to matters of common knowledge.

It is a pity that the late Morris W. Croll never undertook a survey of the present scope. His several articles on the neo-Stoic stylists of the Renaissance and introductory essay (assuming the authorship to be his) to the edition of *Euphues* that he published in collaboration with Harry Clemens in 1916 are, I will venture to say, the most learned and illuminating studies of prose styles to be found anywhere in print. I know of no other scholar who can exhibit a philosophical principle in the very form of a sentence. Croll set a new standard for the study of style, but unfortunately the writings that he lived to complete and publish deal with only two of the five types of style that I have distinguished. The present study is a groping attempt to extend Croll's method to all of the broad types that could be called, as I see it, primary in English prose, both literary and utilitarian.

I am aware that my book is vulnerable. It may be thought that my five "primary" headings are somewhat arbitrary, that I have not adequately supported my argument for the generic kinship of certain subvarieties under one head or another, that I have been tempted into an occasional digression that might have been spared, and that I have expressed some unwelcome opinions. Should these or like objections be raised, I can still hope that my exposition will be found clear as far as it goes and helpful, at worst, for that reason alone.

It is a pleasure for me to make grateful acknowledgement in this place, and in my notes with more precise references, of permission given me by Professor John M. Maguire of the Harvard Law School (emeritus) and Mr. Henry B. Hosmer of Boston to quote from letters of advice concerning the indenture style that they were kind enough to write me; by the *Encyclopaedia Britannica* to quote from H. W. T. Wager's article, "Plants: Cytology" in the thirteenth edition; by Doubleday & Company, Inc., to quote from Arnold Bennett's *How to Live on Twenty-Four Hours a Day* (copyright 1910 by Doran) and from Logan Pearsall Smith's *Trivia* (copyright 1921 by Doubleday, Page); by Mrs. Wyndham Lewis and Methuen & Co. Ltd. to quote from Wyndham Lewis's *The Childermass* (copyright 1928 by Chatto and Windus); by Faber and Faber Ltd. to quote from James Joyce's *Finnegans Wake* (copyright 1939); and by Houghton Mifflin Company to quote from Garrett Mattingly's *The Armada* (copyright 1959).

Long ago I thanked my old friend the late Bernard DeVoto for permission to quote him, given me in a letter dated January 8, 1951, of which the following two paragraphs may be of a certain interest to literary historians and critics generally (Mrs. Bernard DeVoto, as executrix of her husband's estate, has kindly given me permission to quote from this letter):

Little, Brown forwarded to me your request for permission to quote *We Accept with Pleasure*, all rights to which reverted to me, by contract, some years ago. Of course you can quote from it, as much as you'd like to, without fee, & without credit line. This will serve as my permission for you to do so.

Further, my boy, you don't really need to ask permission for such quotes & I am alarmed by the increasing ability of publishers to

PROSE STYLES

bluff people into believing that you do. There are after all innumerable rulings on "reasonable quotation" in critical works. Me, I make a practise of not asking permission, and of never refusing it for anything except outright anthologies.

I take this opportunity to thank numerous other friends whom I have had the advantage of consulting, six of whom were good enough to read either an early or the present version of my work in manuscript, namely Dr. David Erdman, Mrs. Mary Evelyn Blum, Frederick W. Bateson, Herbert Davis, the late E. E. Stoll, and the late W. P. Dunn. And I have learned much about the drafting of legal instruments in conversations with Professors Edward S. Bade, William L. Prosser, Horace E. Read, and Stefan A. Riesenfeld, all sometime of the University of Minnesota Law School.

I began to investigate the present subject systematically during a sabbatical leave of absence from the University of Minnesota in 1946–47, when I enjoyed the additional support of a Fellowship awarded me by the John Simon Guggenheim Memorial Foundation; and I was granted a paid leave of absence again during the fall quarter of 1959–60 by the University of Minnesota for the purpose of completing my manuscript. To both my university and the Guggenheim Foundation I wish to express my deep sense of obligation for the leisure afforded me by their generous help.

H. B.

Minneapolis
January 1, 1966

TABLE OF CONTENTS

Prose Styles

INTRODUCTORY REMARKS

The Terms "Prose" and "Style" Examined

Sweet are the uses of advertisement.   — Mrs. Malaprop

SOMETHING called "prose style" and the styles of various authors, periods, and schools have long been the object of formal study. Here, for a change, is a book about *types* of style: a quite elementary attempt to define, in one short survey, certain universal types whose features — such is the argument — can and ought to be recognized apart from those that mark the school, fashion, period, or individual. The thesis starts from the principle that there is no such thing as prose "style," strictly speaking, only styles, and that insofar as the phrase implies, as it is too often understood to do, something like a single ideal for all varieties of nonmetrical composition, it is pernicious.

That which we take to be characteristic in a work of art or a class of works, we call its style. The critic's problem is to relate effect to cause: to make sure that he actually sees — or hears — a style as well as vaguely senses that it is there.

Talk reaches the ear only as a single file of sounds, and meaning emerges in the hearer's mind only as he recognizes relations in the passing units. Since the units come singly, what they are units of has gone past by the time we recognize it and can never be present to us except as a tissue of memories. A meaning or "impression," once it has taken shape, may remain with us after the details have faded, but the details were its sole source and vehicle. With pictures or buildings we can see the whole and its larger aspects from a distance at which we cannot distinguish details, but with speech the details come first, and if we miss them, we miss everything.

For this reason, when critics describe the style of a plastic or pictorial artefact, they commonly attend first to its larger aspects — its principal masses and outlines — and thereafter to detail, whereas in a literary work they are commonly concerned first with features of the fabric from word to word and phrase to phrase and only thereafter with broader phases of form. These broader phases, indeed, are usually referred to under the term "form," the term "style" being restricted to details of the fabric. The distinction corresponds precisely to that between "cut" and "weave" in the art of the tailor. Our present subject is various "weaves," otherwise styles, as related to various "cuts," otherwise forms or genres, of prose discourse. My purpose is to describe on functional and historical principles a few broad, generic types of style one or another of which, if I am not mistaken, can be identified in virtually every piece of what we call prose.

I should perhaps explain further my insistence that prose — all prose *vis-à-vis* verse — has no one style or character, at least none beyond the negative feature that it is without meter. There follows from this fact, to be sure, a common inference of some importance for my treatment of the "tumbling style" in the fourth chapter below, a style I characterize as "poetical," namely, the idea that a prose writer's thought, unlike that of a poet, is separable from his words and thus patient of being accurately paraphrased or translated. There is some truth in the inference as to prose if it be not too strictly understood, whereas in poetry, thought and word are indeed inseparable. But whatever the difference, the fact remains that prose is a loose, negative category and no proper antithesis to verse — a fact that should be obvious to anyone willing to give a moment's thought to the history of the word "prose," yet a fact of which the significance has been too little understood.

The words "prose" and "verse" are, of course, etymological kin, nor is their etymology in the least obscure. The common, superficially convenient dichotomy, prose-verse, must be supposed to date from the Latin original of our word "prose," the younger of the two terms.[1] This word, used several times by Quintilian (in the phrase "prosa oratio"), but nowhere recorded in Cicero, was explained by the grammarian Donatus as signifying "discourse turned forward," the antithesis of discourse turned as by "cantilena." The "turning" or "bending" force of "cantilena" can, of course, only be meter: "prorsum est porro versum, id est ante versum. Hinc et prorsa oratio, quam non inflexit cantilena." [2] The conception of "discourse turned forward" as opposed to discourse "turned" or "bent" back upon itself in the way of meter — if this is the idea Donatus has in mind — is already misleading; but the confusion dates from the still earlier time when the label was first applied, because the term "prose," in the nature of the case, can only designate a negative idea, namely, discourse that is *not* turned. If we accord the label any positive reference at all, this can only be to the content or thought of the discourse it designates; but to say that the thought of a nonmetrical piece develops or progresses (*i.e.*, is, in that sense, "turned forward") in no way distinguishes it from compositions in verse. How much better if the label had been "nonverse," as we speak of "nonsense," "nonjurors," and the like. The trouble with the ostensibly positive term is, as who can doubt, that it has invited many a rhetorician to grope for a theory of what all prose is or ought to be, notwithstanding the extreme antecedent improbability that all "nonverse" should be found to show common features of a significance comparable to that of meter. It is as if, having singled out all the redheaded men in the world, we should expect to find all the rest blond. Various interesting studies of prose rhythm have appeared in our century, notably those of George Saintsbury and Norton Tempest, and many good things are to be found in books on "prose style," as, for example, those of Sir Herbert Read and Bonamy Dobrée; but none of these excellent writers has accomplished the impossible feat of identifying a single style or genius in all prose, not even in all English prose.[3]

The need for a study along the lines I have followed is apparent if we reflect on how one-sided the approach to style in prose has been from the earliest times.

Rhetoricians have nearly always taught the art of composing one and only one genre and one and only one style, though of course not always the same one. The greatest of the ancient authorities taught the genre and style of full-dress deliberative and forensic argument; and the rhetoricians of Alexandria, whose chief interest was in occasional (or "epideictic") oratory — an expository rather than argumentative form — nevertheless continued to pretend that they were teaching the art of persuasion. So, much later, did the successors of Cicero and Quintilian. We could describe most of the work of the Alexandrian school, along with most of the rhetorics of the Middle Ages, as well-meant misapplications of the excellent ancient rules for deliberative and forensic oratory. The most pedantic and misguided of these authorities are probably the authors of those numerous manuals compiled in the Middle Ages — twenty or more are extant — for the training of legal draftsmen ("scriveners"), under such titles as "ars dictandi" and "ars dictaminis."[4] Persuasion and eloquence are still spoken of in these manuals as the purposes of the trainee; but what has eloquence or persuasion to do with a decree, conveyance, contract, or statement of a diplomatic position, military order, or the like?

It is understandable that the treatises on deliberative and forensic discourse of Aristotle, Cicero, and Quintilian should have been widely influential, even in times when autocrats had abolished or rendered nugatory the institutions of representative government; for, as R. R. Bolgar has recently made clear, both the Hellenistic Greeks and the Romans of the Empire maintained the fiction — the thing later ages have called "the classical tradition" — that they were the heirs and custodians of the art and even the political philosophy of Periclean Athens;[5] and although in the medieval inheritance of classical culture the republican political ideal, which the Caesars had professed to cherish, gave way to that of empire, mere inertia carried over into the medieval schools the main pretensions and many of the rules of the old rhetoric of persuasion.

The system of postclassical ancient rhetoric was formulated by the so-called Second Sophistic school of Alexandria. Scholars are agreed that the chief interest of this school was, as I have said, in occasional oratory and that the main characteristics of Alexandrian prose show the general aim to have been virtuosity or showmanship rather than serious instruction, persuasion, or exhortation. "Individual triumphs were not so much triumphs of individuality as exhibitions of skill in working out a pattern." [6] The pupil composed short, set pieces in a prose calculated primarily to gratify the ear, therefore bristling with the so-called Gorgianic figures — "figures of words" (balance, antithesis, word-play, varieties of repetition, and the like) — as opposed to "figures of thought" (like simile and metaphor).

The reputation of the man after whom the figures of words were named, Gorgias, has been, thanks mainly to Plato's dialogue, that of a facile but shallow controversial speaker and a teacher of rhetoric who did much to corrupt the noble art of public debating. It is important to remember, however, that, as Cicero points out, Gorgias was not himself much engaged in public life,[7] and that he won his fame as a speaker in philosophical rather than political or forensic argumentation and in oratory of the impromptu, occasional sort.[8] The point is that his talent was for argument of the scientific (as opposed to the deliberative and forensic) kind, and that his style was bent to the purpose of this art and displayed those prettifications of it that are conspicuous in the closely related arts of preaching and speechifying for entertainment. The Latin *Rhetorica ad Herennium* remarks of certain of the figures of words — the recurrence of like inflectional or other word endings and word-play — that they "seem more suitable for a speech of entertainment than for use in an actual cause." [9] I shall return to the subject in the third chapter below, but it is important to avoid from the start the possible mistake of supposing that Alexandrian euphuism — or Elizabethan euphuism, for that matter — is a kind of hypertrophied deliberative rhetoric. Rather it is an hypertrophied scientific rhetoric; for what we see beneath its elaborate and exaggerated schematizing is the skeleton of sober expository discourse, a fact alluded to by C. S. Baldwin when he remarks, *à propos* of Alexandrian prose, that "Balance, as an obvious way of marking a comparison or contrast, is so familiar in every language and in every period as hardly to be thought of as a figure. It becomes a figure by becoming a preoccupation . . ." [10]

It would not do for us to imagine that pupils of the Alexandrian teachers had nothing better to do with prose when they went out into the world than make it a pastime or parlor game, forgetting the solid industry of the scholiasts and philosophers whose works swelled the great library. The prose of their treatises was bound, like all expository discourse, to exhibit more or less of schematization, and no doubt some excess of it too, given the influence of the professional rhetoricians; but we should distinguish in our minds between the evidence afforded by the surviving handbooks of rhetoric (like that of Hermogenes) and the actual prose written by a Plotinus or a Ptolemy, a Galen or a Euclid. Any rhetoric, any art, as taught in the schools, where its applications are make believe only, often looks rather silly, as when we read in our French grammar that "The pen of my aunt is under the chair of my cousin." The word "rhetoric," one remembers, was already becoming a bad word in the great days of Athens. Socrates's strictures on the original Sophists are well known; but Aristotle allowed that rhetoric was an indispensable art, even if not very respectable, and proceeded to write the greatest of the Greek manuals of the subject.

In view of the enormous Greek influence on all subsequent European literature, it is important that we should try to form a right idea of the evolution of Greek rhetoric from the pre-Socratics to the Second Sophistic school. We may do well to imagine what the corpus of the prose literature of those times, utilitarian as well as belletristic, would look like lined up in libraries and archives with all the lost texts restored. We may shrewdly suspect that the manuals of rhetoric give only partial and distorted testimony to the kinds of prose actually in circulation. There must have been from very early times a literature of exposition, plenty of occasional oratory (the kind represented by the funeral oration of Pericles), and plenty of official documents (decrees, treaties, diplomatic letters, and the like), as well as the literature of parliamentary and forensic debate that represents the art on which the original Sophists concentrated their teaching. It would then be apparent that the all but exclusive preoc-

[8]

cupation of the schools with the art of debating in the early days, and with occasional oratory later in Alexandria, was by no means the only factor that determined the actual proportions of the different kinds of prose being written.

The teachers of Pericles, Isocrates, and Demosthenes flourished, it would seem, not because the oratory of debate was the only kind of prose of importance in the Athenian scheme of things, but rather because, being virtually indispensable in a community in which every man had sooner or later a part to play in public affairs, it is an art in which competence is rare without benefit of formal training. Later, when the democracy gave way to a series of autocratic governments, culminating in that of the Alexandrian empire, election to office as a legislator no longer offered a career to the citizen. Pleading in the courts became increasingly technical,[11] therefore deviating in style more and more from forensic eloquence toward cool exposition. Hence, many men who would once have made eager pupils of the teachers of practical debating would now be studying a different kind of rhetoric in order to prepare themselves suitably for bureaucratic offices or scholarship.

The art of expression practised by public administrators appearing before popular audiences is not that of deliberative argument; it is didactic. Scholars teach; spokesmen, especially the spokesmen of autocratic governments, preach. Neither argues; both assert; and both, almost of necessity, make conspicuous use of the same *schemata verborum*. The preacher displays his wit and sweetens his propositions for the ear by emphasizing the element of balance or symmetry inherent in all propositions of the form subject-copula-predicate; but propositions of this form are precisely those most central to the prose of the scholar and teacher.

Antonius, in Cicero's dialogue *De Oratore*, speaks at one point as if dissatisfied with the traditional rhetoricians' neglect of the non-deliberative and non-forensic forms of discourse. The rhetoricians, he says, supply no rules for the composition of history, works of instruction, exhortation, consolation, or warning, or "the abstract sort of inquiry, unrelated to times or persons" (presumably what we should call the scientific monograph).[12] But he ends by persuading himself that the standard schooling in deliberative and forensic argumentation is good enough after all and expresses his belief in the full competence of the man trained in the standard discipline to handle any kind of discourse he may be called on to compose.[13] Antonius's conclusion may be said to represent the view that has been dominant throughout the Western world from the days of the Greek *polis* to the twentieth century, and it is a view by no means difficult to account for. The training of the orator prescribed by the ancient masters amounted to a broad educational program, and the genre that its rules were made for — the harangue by word of mouth before a jury or a legislature, the *professed* aim of postclassical rhetoric generally, as I have said — is probably as near to being the type of all good prose discourse as one could name — so near and yet so far. Whether any improvement over the old discipline has yet been or is likely soon to be effected may be a question; but the principle it has mostly tended in practice to inculcate (in spite of the reservations of its best exponents), that there is one best style for all purposes, can hardly be defended. The long persistence of this fallacy can only be attributed to inertia in the teaching profession. Heaven knows it is easier to teach one art than two or more, especially when only one is treated in the available handbooks.

Problems of style have been considered with more discrimination by the critics than by the rhetoricians, but even the critics need to be read with caution. Thomas Gray, for example, who was certainly a good critic, makes this modest confession concerning a passage of his own prose: "What Tacitus has said in five words, I imagine I have said in fifty. Such is the misfortune of imitating the inimitable." [14] Taken strictly the remark is acceptable enough, for if one is to imitate Tacitus, one must indeed be brief; yet it more than half implies that brevity is absolutely better than copiousness — the opposite of the "Ciceronian" principle and no less mistaken if understood as a universal rule. How often we read that an author is too this or that — too formal, loose, elaborate, or whatever — where we can only guess at a right standard of judgement. And how often we meet an oracular prescription, especially in the older authorities, like this of Matthew Arnold: "The needful qualities for a fit prose are regularity, uniformity, precision, balance . . ."[15] But a fit prose for what purpose? Would such a prose have any place in *Tristram Shandy* or an essay of Charles Lamb?

To make an end of our faultfinding, literary historians, too, are sometimes disappointing, though it is not so often because of what they say as of what they omit. Paying too little attention to broad differences of style according to function, they sometimes miss the rationale of a passing fashion in style; and they are often so preoccupied with describing the fashion of a given age — always, of course, a belletristic fashion — that they allow us to forget the unfashionable kinds of prose contemporaneously current. It would be an exaggeration, of course, to say that all of the broad types of style I am about to describe have been in use in every period of history, yet not so very wide of the truth at that. If the fashion or fashions of each generation are to be understood, they must be observed with reference to differing requirements of communication — requirements which have differed in the same essential ways over long stretches of time. I can say with confidence that each of the types I shall distinguish has a long history of its own and that the historians, by omitting to give enough attention to the simultaneous currency of different primary types of style, have missed the best approach to a philosophical definition of each.

The idea of euphuism as a humanistic style, generally accepted before the Croll-Clemens edition of *Euphues* in 1916, illustrates the kind of error resulting from too little regard to the timeless rationale of this prose and a too nearsighted preoccupation with the moving current of the historical process. Croll showed that it was, rather, a style in the tradition of medieval didactic prose in Latin; yet not even Croll brought out the point that the ultimate explanation of the mechanics of it is to be sought in something more central than medieval didacticism or pedantry or even Alexandrian rhetoric, namely, in the very nature of authentic science; so that the history of the style in its generic character is truly a phase of the history of science itself. Again, historians of seventeenth-century literature, although they often deal learnedly with the polite "Senecans" from Bacon to the Restoration and thereupon with new influences in the prose of the age of reason, often ignore altogether the magnificent oratory of the Long Parliament, which is hardly to be matched by anything of the kind in earlier English prose. Is there any reason to neglect as literature the oratory of Eliot, Pym, or Cromwell, when every literary history of England makes its bow to that of Edmund Burke? And although literary histories, at least the longer ones, give some place to historiography, which of them so much as mentions the style of the scrivener?

I cannot pretend that the divisions of style I have made are more than vaguely parallel. Ideally, we should begin with the whole range of literature and work down step by step to kinds of discourse of increasing particularity, each bifurcation being made according to a single criterion. But one has only to put the notion into words to give it up as illusory. *Objets d'art* can be usefully grouped in different ways for different purposes; I would claim for my types of prose style only that they are nearly enough parallel to be mutually illuminating. My concern is to show in each an important element of homogeneity different from that in each of the others and to test the argument by drawing various comparisons and contrasts. Only omniscience, I believe, could place them in strict genealogical or evolutionary relations.

Each of these varieties, as I shall try to show, answers to the conditions of a certain type of transaction whose importance in the human comedy causes it to get repeated over and over and thus standardized. As I count the determining types of transaction, they are remarkably few, all told.

One is the bid of the politician or lawyer to win the assent of a deliberative assembly (an election crowd, a legislature, a jury) to a position which, for various reasons, he cannot establish by means of a strictly scientific argument and which, therefore, he must defend by appealing mainly to the political, moral, or religious predispositions of his audience. It is convenient to name the style of this kind of speaker the "deliberative," though the term is commonly used in a narrower sense which differentiates it from the "forensic" (on which see pp. 26–27).

Another is the strict, orderly treatise or lesson, whether ratiocinative or merely descriptive, spoken or written, the style of which we shall call simply the "expository."

Another is prophecy. Prophecy is an oracular piece of instruction or warning, bold and dogmatic, often highly diffuse, sometimes seemingly addressed to one or a very few persons whose near presence is acknowledged by more or less use of the second personal pronoun, sometimes seemingly broadcast as if to the world at large and over the heads of any near bystanders: the kind of lesson taught seriously by the Old Testament prophets and moderns like Francis Bacon or Thomas Carlyle and in a light vein by numerous essayists of the last hundred and fifty years.

Yet another is the colloquial, rough-and-ready storytelling and haranguing by the wit in homespun and his modern American city counterpart in journalism. This style is not so ancient, at least in the prose of extant documents, as the others named so far; but its genealogy can be traced to the style of preliterate Germanic poetry. It is the "tumbling" style, the only style native to English literature, for all the others are accountable, directly or indirectly, to ancient Greco-Roman influence.[16]

Fifth and last come two kinds of transaction, both very old, of which was born the "indenture" style. One was the communication of a formal message by letter; the other, the ancient Roman "nexum," the thing Sir Henry Maine identified as the standard form of ceremony in early Roman civilization for conveyance, adoption, and marriage. The "nexum" originally involved no document; but, in time, a written record of the proceedings came into use and was accorded legal weight, and its modern descendant is the so-called "objective" type of legal instrument, the one in which the parties to the transaction are spoken of in the third person. But practically all instruments in the modern world begin with a greeting and end with the signatures of the authors, features indicating the dominant influence of the diplomatic letter.

Of the five kinds of prose named so far, three — the deliberative, the expository, and the prophetic — are essentially non-narrative. They do not, unless incidentally, recount events in time. Tumbling discourse seems essentially a narrative kind, to judge by what we know of its history. One can only surmise that its insistent, energetic accentuation, like the later gallop of the ballad fourteener, was the inevitable response of the muse to the storytelling impulse, and that this impulse was the one which, more than any other, demanded expression in verse in the heroic period, and in a not dissimilar prose later on.

Official documents too are narrative, for every one of them sets forth, in the present tense, an "act" or "deed." The scrivener's style, as we shall notice in the sixth chapter, is recognizable in some features of medieval and early modern historiography, but later historians, with good reason, came to abhor and eschew its influence. Where the influence is apparent in the narrative prose of modern times, it is only for special effects.

The question whether there is such a thing as a style generic to narrative discourse naturally arises. My answer, given the sense in which I conceive the term "generic," is no, unless in the one respect that its vocabulary usually contains a greater variety of verbs than any of the non-narrative kinds. In a passage already cited from Cicero's *De Oratore* (p. 9), Antonius makes the more general remark about history that "for fluency and diversity of diction it comes first" ("Haud scio an flumine orationis et varietate maximum").[17] But history, being the only kind of narrative prose that the great ancient authorities have anything to say about, was pretty much an orphan, rhetorically speaking. Antonius follows the remark just quoted by saying, "nowhere do I find this art [historiography] supplied with any independent directions from the rhetoricians." In the *Orator*, Cicero likens the style of history to the kind I designate in the third chapter the "expository" — the one he has found characteristic of the Sophists.[18] Quintilian advises the student of oratory to read history, but warns him against history as a model of style on the ground that "it borders closely on poetry." [19] These and other ancient writers refer fairly often to the art of historiography, but both the ancients and the many modern authorities on the subject are concerned mostly with subject matter rather than style, and when they do speak of style, it is not in terms germane to our purpose.

The best theory I can offer is that narrative prose runs to varieties marked by the prevailing features of one or another of the non-narrative kinds, mainly two. The style of what we may call standard history and fiction is, on the whole, that of deliberative discourse, and the only notable deviation from this is in the way of what I call the "prophetic." A third style one might mention in passing would be the expository — the kind Cicero thought represented by all history, as we have seen — but I find it only in narratives of the euphuistic tradition, which are a kind of freak, and, as it were by accident, in such records as a mariner's logbook or the *Anglo-Saxon Chronicle*. I say "by accident" in this last-mentioned kind of record because this consists of mere brief notations of fact made from day to day or year to year according to no strict principle governing the inclusion or exclusion of material; it exhibits the semblance of a style only when, and insofar as, the writer in making a series of entries confines himself, whether for practical reasons or inertia, to one type of matter and so repeats given forms of expression. In the repetition of such forms we seem to see the same conscious schematizing of the prose as in strict expository discourse; but at any point the matter and style may take a new turn, as perhaps where a new writer takes up the pen, and thus exhibit no more strictly homogeneous or functional a character as a whole than we are likely to find in a random conversation. My further notice of narrative styles (other than the "tumbling" and the "indenture") will accordingly be included in the second, third, and fifth chapters.

A final word of caution. In talking about style in prose one is seldom free from the discomfort of uncertainty as to how much of the thing one is minded to call a style may elude his capacity to define in objective terms. We may be able to discover a meaning in one or two characteristic features of a piece of writing and then find nothing more to say. Have we then defined "a style"? The nature of our subject is that of eternally unfinished business. There would not seem to be any harm in designating as "a style" something of which we can furnish only a meager description. The term, like the word "character," its near synonym, is extremely flexible and should not be misleading to anyone who will bear in mind the enormous neutral or variable element present in most objects to which people attribute a style or character, whether persons or things. The neutral or variable element is minimal in such a thing as an heraldic device or a military uniform, every detail of which is rigidly prescribed; but at the other end of the scale, where most prose literature lies, this element is very large indeed. The two considerations to remember are, first, that a strong impression of character or style in a piece of prose may be given by a mere hint or two, as it may in a person by nothing more than the angle of his cigar or his hat, and, second, that no critic can hope to describe any style exhaustively. It is more important, if I am not mistaken, that our definitions should each have a center than that they should be elaborately full, the more so since we are concerned only with broad types and not, unless incidentally, with subtypes or individual variations.

What we want for present purposes is to characterize each of our generic styles as marked by a very few ways of expression more important to its business than others that may appear in any typical text, noting, where possible, some one way that can be seen as the all but exact outward form of its essential function and as more or less productive of the other features of the style. Thus in expository prose the equation is certainly the characteristic expression, having two parts (subject and predicate-substantive or predicate-adjective) whose balanced position corresponds to the equivalence of the ideas that the words stand for and invites the writer to emphasize this equivalence by making the aforesaid sentence members resemble each other in form as closely as possible.

To summarize the whole book in a single paragraph: the genius of deliberative writing seems to me to show itself most characteristically in a highly organic, climactic movement; that of exposition in the form of the equation and in series of parallel terms, which often exhibit some common element of form; that of prophecy in bold, loosely connected, terse, paradoxical aphorisms; that of tumbling prose in a crowded stress-patterning reminiscent of that of alliterative-accentual verse, though a characteristic diction in this style is almost as near its center; and that of the traditional indenture in the stretching of a single sentence to include the whole contents of the document. These I take to be the principal ways in which the debater, and likewise the "standard" historian or novelist, makes his case compelling; the scientist or philosopher and the teacher, preacher, or occasional orator, and likewise the writer of a log or the barest of annals, make their discourse clear, orderly, catchy, and easy to remember; the prophet or the narrative writer of the cryptic kind speaks "as one having authority"; the "tumbling" writer, like a professional strong man, puts on a display, commonly with much clowning, of literary muscularity; and the draftsman of indentures sets forth, or tries to set forth, the "act" or "deed" of a given party or given parties in all of its possible or imaginable implications with microscopic precision and, at the same time, the tightest possible grammatical unity.

THE DELIBERATIVE STYLE

The Style of Persuasion

Vivit? Immo vero etiam in senatum venit . . .
— Cicero, *In L. Cat.* I

IT IS no wonder, as I have already remarked, that the kind of prose composition taught by Aristotle, Cicero, and Quintilian has been widely supposed, though mistakenly, to be absolutely the best kind — mistakenly, since there can hardly be any one absolutely best kind of prose or poetry, any more than of food or drink. But certain it is that skill in persuasion is a skill of high value to all men; many of the virtues of a good deliberative argument are also the virtues of a good story; and often in describing an object or explaining a technical process to nonexperts, one may find it more effective to present what one has to say in the same kind of highly organized form and common, nontechnical language that one would use for a deliberative plea than to trust to the merely technical, comparatively diffusive form that might do for accuracy and clarity if one were addressing experts.

Thanks to the fact that most of the principles of good writing that the modern generations have been taught in school and college are those that Cicero and Quintilian standardized for the training of the pleader at the bar and the parliamentary orator, a rather brief description of the deliberative style should suffice in this place.

The two great Roman authorities pointed out the advantage of dividing a discourse into fairly distinct sections and of disposing

[18]

these in a certain order; [1] they gave considerable thought to the best order in which to present different kinds of evidence or other support; [2] they called for common and pure (as opposed to recondite and inelegant) diction; [3] and they insisted on copiousness of expression. [4]

If we attend to these prescriptions and observe further the great care Cicero takes in his own speeches with the organization of his sentences and paragraphs and with his transitions and other means of forward and backward reference to knit the whole firmly together, we have as nearly a universal scheme for the orderly presentation of any subject that may be at all complicated as could perhaps be imagined. Where, if anywhere, does the scheme come short of universal usefulness?

The rule of "cōpie" or copiousness, for one thing, is well enough when one is addressing an audience by word of mouth, for the obvious reason that oral discourse is difficult at best to follow, and most difficult of all for persons having no special knowledge of the subject under discussion; therefore this rule is excellent for argumentation in a legislature or before a jury. But one who has got into the habit of expressing himself copiously may find himself at a serious disadvantage in writing, say, an article for a learned journal or like organ where space is at a premium; and the old rule has tempted many a writer, and speaker as well, so to fall in love with his own fluency as to turn into an intolerable bore.

Other features typical of deliberative speeches that are proper enough on the rostrum or the hustings or at the bar but out of place elsewhere are the large space commonly devoted to extolling the speaker's own virtues and the repeated expressions of his deference to his audience. A measure of self-advertisement that would otherwise be unbecoming can be a virtue in a politician or other pleader for the assent of an assembly, for this person may have to depend to no small degree upon public recognition of his reputation. He may need to boast unashamedly of his accomplishments if he is to inspire people's confidence in the wisdom of his present position. [5] And he may appropriately emphasize his respect for his hearers in terms that would otherwise seem fulsome, for in free societies the will of

the many is sovereign and more likely when great issues are at stake
— such is human nature — to be bent by an appeal graced with the
arts of courtship than one stripped to its rational content. A speaker
flatters his audience by making a refrain of the appropriate vocative,
whatever it be ("Patres conscripti," "My Lords," "Lords and Com-
mons of England"), and by such devices as the rhetorical question
and the parenthesis, which, by suggesting the give-and-take of debate, keep reminding each hearer that his opinion, whatever it be,
will weigh in the final accounting. Vox populi, vox Dei.

One phase of good deliberative prose should be brought out more
prominently than it is by the original authorities. This is what we
may call the principle of climax. Not only do good orators take
care in presenting arguments of different weight in a suitable order,
but they also like to sub- or super-ordinate every point they make
to neighboring ones. They often underline what they are up to by
using several sentence members of tapered length (from long to
short or short to long), sometimes with correlatives, or a repeated
key word, for extra force ("plenum est forum, plena templa circum
forum, pleni omnes aditus huius templi ac loci"). In deliberative
argument, subordinating constructions are prominent, and the tendency is to avoid rather than parade mechanical likenesses between
such expressions of corresponding or parallel order as may occur.
The purpose is not only to enforce the idea (or illusion) that each
part of the discourse has only one right place in the whole, but to
convey as strongly as possible the feeling of a constant progress. The
varying constructions suggest variety in the passing thought (as if it
were landscape being seen by a passing traveler). Thus they inevitably suggest motion. It is misleading to speak, as one of the critics
has done, of Cicero's "balanced orotundity." [6] Balance — at least the
exact balancing of the outward form of sentences or sentence members — is the way of formal exposition. By contrast, Cicero and all
good deliberative speakers go out of their way to vary the getup of
successive paragraphs, sentences, and parts of sentences, as if to suggest that they are constantly breaking new ground and making headway across it. Quintilian may be referring to this principle when he
says of Domitius Afer that he "was so little disposed to be studious

of the nice and delicate gratifications of melody, that, even when harmony presented itself, he would put something in the way to interrupt it." [7] With this kind of variation and by a liberal use of cross-reference, often some distance forward or backward, the speaker gives us both the sense that we are in motion and assurance that he is mindful of his direction and destination.

A good deliberative argument is a carefully timed performance. Unlike a work of exposition, which allows, indeed often invites, the reader to pause and study some part of it at his leisure, a deliberative argument gives the illusion of a controlled, generally increasing momentum, and its effect can be ruined by an interruption. The speaker uses every possible means to jog our attention — exclamations, apostrophes, questions, gestures — and to spur us ever forward, not only with series of tapered expressions but also by means of stimulating suspensions. The beginning of the periodic sentence, which is commonly understood to be the typical — at least the most important — unit of deliberative expression, is, by definition, some kind of subordinate sentence member, typically a subordinate clause, and Cicero's prose, as we know, is full of parentheses. Our speaker's purpose is not so much to induce or enable us to remember the parts of his argument as to inspire us to cast a favorable vote when hands are to be counted: *movere* rather than *docere*. He may warn us, indeed, that time is running out. Each part of his speech is carefully machined to fit the context at one and only one place, and exerts its full force only there. It does not ordinarily, like so many of the propositions that make up scientific theorems, convey a self-contained meaning when cited in isolation.

Of the diction of deliberative prose, we need only remark that, except for the production of occasional bold, special effects, it runs to the conservative, the literal, and the abstract. It is conservative (avoiding, that is, all words of limited currency, such as technical terminology, dialect, and slang) in order that its appeal may reach the widest possible variety of listeners; literal rather than figurative both for the sake of perspicuity and lest the speaker lay himself open to suspicions of depending more on artifice or fancy than on truth and reason; and abstract inasmuch as the important premises of arguments about great public issues are usually political or moral principles rather than material facts. Much of the jargon of parliamentary and judicial procedure is, of course, tedious ("tentative findings of the interim committee," "the matter was taken under advisement," "Mr. Chairman, I rise to a point of order"); but good speakers avoid getting bogged down in it and make the most of abstract terms that are highly charged with emotion ("honor," "treason," "liberty," "death") and of terms for the superlative, the categorical, and the unique (in one of Cicero's speeches we find "all bitterness, all pains and tortures"; "the chief assistance of all nations"; "the common refuge of all men"; "most bitter distress"; "this most lovely country"; "all Italy"; "whatever fortune"; "the express appointment of fate").[8]

Deliberative oratory is presumably as old as civilization. Deliberation on matters of common interest by any group of people, with its implication of the authority of the majority as superior to that of any single member, whether the group be official or casual, large or small, may be seen as the very kernel of democracy. So long as each member of the group acknowledges and defers to the will of a majority of the membership, no matter how ruthlessly the group may choose, if it be not coextensive with the whole community, to impose its will upon other people, we may properly speak of democracy within the group; and it is this democracy in which the art of deliberative argument originated and has evolved. Needless to say, however, the art has attained its highest development only among what we know as the great free communities — those in which the spirit of government by the consent of the governed has permeated the whole people: Periclean Athens, Republican Rome, and the great modern democratic states.

Distrust of eloquence by scientists and philosophers dates from very early. Already in democratic Athens, Socrates, and soon Aristotle, spoke disparagingly of the actual oratory of their times as if it were mainly an art of trickery and mainly employed for imposing upon the vulgar and the ignorant;[9] and derogatory opinions of eloquence in the modern world have been expressed by Francis Bacon, by early members of the Royal Society, and often by commentators in the twentieth century.[10] A quite typical illustration of recent skepticism would be an American book entitled *The Art of Plain Talk*.[11]

This title indeed expresses the point of view of all the skeptics of eloquence. Their ideal is fidelity to philosophical or scientific truth, and they fancy that language can be found to express this kind of truth with something near to mathematical precision and without resort to any special art in the use of words. They are mistaken, of course, forgetting that the relation between thought and expression is a very different thing within closed systems like Euclidean geometry or formal logic from what it is outside. We may properly speak of perfect precision in solving problems within such systems, but never in the expressing of experience — not even in experimental science, for here, terms being one thing and ideas or things another, art in the use of language is indispensable.

The skeptics are right enough in objecting to rhetoricians who use their art for evil ends, but they forget that there are other truths besides those of logic and physical science, and that it takes more than the truth to make a civilization.

The problem of the deliberative speaker, a different one from that of the writer of formal exposition, is a problem of the future. It is that of *predicting the effect* of the decision for which he pleads and making this the crucial ground of his argument. But the effect of a decision affecting human affairs is something nobody can foresee with anything approaching the accuracy of typical predictions in the more exact of the sciences. The speaker's calculations involve two highly variable unknowns: first, the character of the agents (they may include the whole community) upon whom will depend the execution of the recommended decision, if it is voted, and, second, the speaker's own eloquence, considered as an influence outlasting the occasion of the speech and hence as a factor affecting the performance of these agents. The problem is not really one of calculation at all, but rather that of creative leadership.

The speaker's appeal may be for a morally noble action where the odds may be doubtful and doubt openly acknowledged that the action will prove advantageous from the worldly point of view. Such was the kind of appeal Winston Churchill made to his people when they were threatened with invasion by the Germans in 1940. An older example, and one in which the chief addressee saw, as he explicitly tells us, the speaker's eloquence as a promising factor in the execution of the program advocated, is a speech of Nestor in the second *Iliad*. Nestor argues before Agamemnon and his council, in obedience, he says, to the will of Zeus, for a renewed effort in the war. He stresses the fact, to be sure, that the omens are favorable, but the fray, he fears, will be violent, and he concedes that it is uncertain "whether the promise of aegis-bearing Zeus be a lie or no." He wonders whether, if defeat come, it will not be owing to "the baseness of thy warriors" as well as to "their ill skill in battle." The essential appeal, like that of Winston Churchill, is honor and hope, not predictable success; yet a practical, even military efficacy in its force is seen by the king, who says in reply, "Ah, father Zeus and Athene and Apollo, would that among the Achaians I had ten such councillors; then would the city of king Priam soon bow beneath our hands, captive and wasted." [12]

I believe investigation would show that most of those deliberative speeches of the past that have come to stand in people's minds as masterpieces of eloquence are ones in which the case has been made to pivot upon some lofty moral or political principle rather than upon facts. When facts are the chief matter of debate, deliberative speeches tend to resemble technical treatises. A fact can be established by evidence, and the substance of evidence adduced to prove a fact counts for more than the form in which either the fact or the supporting evidence is stated. Not so with principles.

Consider any of numerous statements of principle in Burke's speech *On Conciliation with America*. "Public calamity," he says "is a mighty leveller." [13] It would have been proper for a sociologist to play down the emotional implications of the idea for the sake of scientific accuracy. He might say, "Events that seriously injure all or most of the membership of a community tend to bring them all around to a common political point of view." But the very virtue of this statement as science renders it unsuitable for purposes of persuasion. Burke is advancing an idea too simple to need stating in pedestrian terms, and is urging not so much its truth as its importance. "Calamity," though an abstract word, does much more toward evoking the feelings men experience in the presence of floods, conflagrations, massacres, and the like, than the more analytical expression, "events that seriously injure, etc."; and the phrase "mighty leveller" is a striking metaphor. It is as if the abstraction "public calamity" had suddenly turned into the giant Talus and were visibly beating down a concourse of people with his flail. Notice a like personification in "refined policy has ever been the parent of confusion," and figurative language that is hardly less interesting in "genuine simplicity of heart is a healing and cementing principle." [14]

But metaphor is not indispensable, for aphorisms tend to be short and often owe much of their force to their brevity alone. They may also pack the weight of strong authority by means of allusion. American politicians can always count on a lively response by borrowing a phrase from the Gettysburg Address, and English politicians can, or could within living memory, quote a Latin tag to good effect. So Burke, "abeunt studia in mores," "spoliatis arma supersunt," [15] and the like.

So intimate is the connection between principles and eloquence that not only can a skilful speaker make principles prevail against the force of adverse practical considerations (Nestor, Churchill), but many speakers, even when practical considerations are in their favor, go out of their way to invoke principles as the most compelling of all arguments.

But facts are compelling too, provided they be easy to convey and establish. Deliberative speakers, we find, make the most of facts that are well known, thus reminding us that eloquence is rather the art of shaping an argument out of familiar cloth than anything like instruction, least of all instruction in difficult or novel matters. Burke's speech contains many passages like the following:

The House has gone further; it has declared conciliation admissible, previous to any submission on the part of America.

This, sir, is, I believe, about the true number [of the inhabitants of the colonies]. There is no occasion to exaggerate, where plain truth is of so much weight and importance. But whether I put the present numbers too high or too low, is a matter of little moment . . .

As to the wealth which the colonies have drawn from the sea by their fisheries, you had all that matter fully opened at your bar . . .

. . . on this point of taxes the ablest pens and most eloquent tongues have been exercised . . .

. . . we thought, sir, that the utmost which the discontented colonists could do, was to disturb authority. We never dreamed they could of themselves supply it . . .[16]

And sometimes we meet propositions that appear to combine the weight of fact with the weight of principle. Burke, like Cicero, often puts commonplaces in such a way as to make them look like statements of particular fact, as, for example, "I pardon something to the spirit of liberty"; "I cannot alter the nature of man"; "He [the Turkish Sultan] governs with a loose rein that he may govern at all."[17]

It is of the greatest interest to notice that Burke thinks it necessary to apologize for that one part of his speech in which he introduces exact and extensive statistics, and to observe the terms of his apology. "I choose, sir," he says, "to enter into these minute and particular details, because generalities, which in all other cases are apt to heighten and raise the subject, have here a tendency to sink it. When we speak of commerce with our colonies, fiction lags after truth; invention is unfruitful, and imagination cold and barren."[18] He is, in other words, making an exception to the implied postulate that deliberative eloquence is typically a matter of generalities, of fiction, of invention, of imagination.

Our chapter is entitled "The Deliberative Style," and a word must be said about the closely related kind of speaking known as forensic. It is convenient to regard the forensic speech as near kin to the deliberative: one which may be eloquent in much the same way, but which also may and often does veer far toward cool, formal exposition.

The theoretical difference is that the deliberative speaker typically looks to the future; the forensic to the past. The typical problem of the pleader at the bar is to make relevant statements of fact, proving the crucial fact or facts by invoking other facts as evidence. Now prominent among relevant statements of fact are statements of law; law, according to traditional theory, whether written or unwritten, is fact: it is not, like political or moral doctrine, merely articulated aspiration toward ideals of the good or the beautiful. But the facts of a case at law (like all other facts) belong to the past (the court is in theory bound absolutely by them in finding its verdict, regardless of the consequences); whereas moral and political axioms are timeless, stimulating, and expansive, and any proposal for their better realization, though it may be urged as the conclusion of an argument resting upon them as if they were law, looks to the future.

Obviously in cases where facts are the sole grounds of the pleader's position, clear evidence forthcoming to establish these facts, and the rules of evidence unambiguous as to the conclusions to be drawn, the problem is reduced to that of formal exposition. Some cases are indeed extremely cut-and-dried and elicit little or nothing in the way of eloquence; but no problem of legal administration is commoner or more challenging than that of interpretation, and it has long been recognized that to interpret law is to make law. Law cannot always be found by the simple kind of research that finds facts; and a court having to interpret law becomes, in reality, a legislature.[19] When it does, the forensic speaker may have the same opportunity and the same need to speak eloquently as the deliberative.

Any full history of the style we have been describing would have to take account of much besides the literature of deliberative and forensic oratory proper, notably the written argumentation that we meet in books, pamphlets, and the editorial pages of newspapers.

Good deliberative arguments for oral delivery are naturally somewhat more formal than those written to be read. Orations tend to be more "copious" and more emphatically to acknowledge in various ways the living presence of the audience. Orators commonly give more prominence to their initial salutations and more often interject vocatives as they proceed, and they are more inclined to make use, for theatrical effect, of rhetorical questions, apostrophes, suspensions, and inversions of word order than would be suitable to the printed page.

It may seem strange that the different requirements of spoken and written argumentation were not better understood by the Renaissance Ciceronians, whose writings have become a byword of stilted affectation.

Erasmus criticizes by name over a hundred Ciceronians of various nations, mainly for their pedantry in the matter of vocabulary and diction, and also, though not quite in so many words, takes exception to the excessive *copia* of one of them, Christophe de Longueil.[20] This writer delivered an elaborate and lengthy defense of himself in a certain academic debate at Rome concerning his fitness to receive the honor of Roman citizenship, and Erasmus finds it a gross example of much ado about a small matter. Bacon specifically deplores the "affectionate [meaning "affected"] study of eloquence and copie of speech" that the humanists brought in, and cites "the flowing and watery vein of Osorius, the Portugal bishop" by way of illustration.[21] My firsthand knowledge of the writings of these Ciceronians is slight indeed, but still sufficient to make me wonder whether any comparable corpus of literature could make drearier reading, for it is everywhere blown up with the flatulence of handbook exercises, of which the ideal could be described as that of laboring the obvious in the most solemn manner possible. For a characteristic single example of these exercises I would cite an argument for the affirmative in an imaginary debate on the question "Is it good to marry?" to be found in *The Foundacion of Rhetorike* of Richard Rainolde (London, 1563).[22] It runs to twelve printed octavo pages; it cites familiar passages of Scripture, mythology, and history relating to marriage; it refutes the feeblest and most artificial of objections; sentence after sentence is swollen with pairs and triplets of synonyms; and the inversions of word order and the tone of voice throughout indicate that it is got up for platform delivery. And here is Erasmus's description of de Longueil's oration:

De Longueil treated with utmost seriousness this plainly ridiculous charge [that he had dared to compare France favorably with Italy, etc., etc.], manifesting a truly wonderful pomp of words, a great show of talent, the greatest vehemence, at times much urbanity, using the age of Cicero just as the author of "The Battle of Frogs and Mice" made use, in sport, of the Homeric Iliad, fitting to frogs and mice and equally ridiculous things the splendid words and deeds of gods, goddesses, and heroes. He exaggerated the danger of his position, picturing armed cohorts and bands of gladiators by whom the authority of the Senate and the free action of the law had been hindered. He set before them in fancy early Rome, the Queen of the World, and Romulus with his *Quirites* as her guard and protector; then the Common People and the ruling Senate, the people divided into classes and tribes, the Praetorian right, the veto of the Tribunes; he pictured provinces, colonies, towns, allies of the Seven-hilled City; he quoted a decree of the Senate; he cited laws: — I marvel that he did not remember the water-clocks, nine of which I think are allowed to the defendant. Next the emotions were called into play; the old statesmen of the Roman Republic were appealed to and summoned forth from their tombs.[23]

The imitators more often take Cicero's orations for their model than his letters or other comparatively informal pieces. But, of course, the Renaissance was a battleground of ideas. Innovations nearly always arouse opposition, and nothing was newer or more controversial in the age of the humanists than humanism itself in its many phases or, somewhat later, the new science. Men who had inherited the contentious tradition of Scholastic philosophy and discovered the masterly controversial art of Cicero were bound to be emulous of this; and it is a commonplace that even in Cicero's correspondence and other non-oratorical pieces the style is often redolent of the platform. Hence it is no wonder that the doctrinaire Ciceronians seldom condescend to anything so informal as the style that distinguishes genial eclectics like Erasmus and Sir Thomas More.

The applause of listening senates to command can be no proper motive of debaters in an age in which senates do not exist; and the affectation of the more ceremonious graces of Cicero's oratory by writers addressing the public only through books must be set down to the combination of their exaggerated faith in the power of the written word alone and their undeveloped taste. They evidently believed that the force of Cicero's style resided wholly in the words and the subject without reference to the character of the addressee or the conditions of the communication. Yet perhaps their faith was not altogether misplaced. Manners are presumably better exaggerated than neglected, and one can hardly doubt that the study of

Cicero in action as champion of freedom and justice by the Renaissance men, whatever the kind of government to which they gave their actual allegiance and whatever the causes they espoused (Marc Antoine Muret delivered a notorious oration in defense of the Massacre of St. Bartholomew),[24] contributed in the long run very substantially to the evolution of what we call today the free world.

Let me repeat the generalization that many of the virtues of a good deliberative argument are also virtues of a good story. But we can go further. It could be said that every story, historical or imagined, as opposed to a mere logbook or chronicle, is in the nature of a deliberative argument (the idea is very properly brought to mind by the fact that in the not distant past it was possible to speak indifferently of the "argument" of a story and the "argument" put forward by a debater).

The absence of an argument in a chronicle gives a peculiarly strong impression of its truth, an effect we recognize in primitive mythology. In typical versions of the ancient myths, the event is seen as if it had been handed on by an original witness innocent of any selective or critical intention and therefore peculiarly reliable.

The line dividing this kind of record from the storytelling of the novelist or historian is not easy to draw, since, on the one hand, no witness can be supposed perfectly innocent of art and, on the other, novelists and historians always pretend that their stories are true; but we may draw it in theory by saying that in standard history and fiction the writer controls the story and in the chronicle kind of narrative he is controlled by it.

The great myths have a place in our culture quite different from that of sophisticated history or fiction. Their place is like that of day and night or the flowers of the field. The difference is not in the presence or absence of art in the teller, but in his point of view. The mythographer's art, as we see it in a story like that of Jacob and Esau, is surely supreme, but he begins with no preamble and ends with no formal conclusion. He is ostensibly concerned only to retail various *res gestae* as they were told to him. The Old Testament writers were inspired, of course, by the ulterior motive of piety, and scholars recognize that the priests of the Second Temple put the canon together to exhibit a large historico-theological pattern. But the pattern is nowhere fully and plainly summarized and is not easy for the unlearned reader to perceive. The story of Jacob and Esau, a quite typical episode, gives no indication that either the original writer or writers or the priestly compiler weighed possible alternatives before deciding to tell this particular story or that they were consciously aiming at calculated effects. It begins with the noncommittal formula "and it came to pass," and it has no clearly marked end (Jacob's departure for Padan-aram and sojourn with Laban is continuous with the deception of Isaac and Esau by Rebekah and Jacob, and the division of the text into readings or "lessons" decided upon by the Anglican Church does not coincide with the canonical chapter divisions).

With this kind of narrative, whose art is so largely concealed — perhaps unconscious — we may contract the sophisticated kind wherein the writer quite consciously and openly defines and develops a theme, often announcing it at the very beginning: "The wrath sing, goddess, of Peleus' son Achilles"; "Thucydides [speaking of himself in the third person], an Athenian, wrote the [i.e., this] history of the war between the Peloponnesians and the Athenians, beginning at the moment that it broke out, and believing that it would be a great war, and more worthy of relation than any that had preceded it"; and consider likewise the wording of many a famous title, such as *The Decline and Fall of the Roman Empire*; *The History of Tom Jones, A Foundling*; *Great Expectations*; and the like.

Having announced his theme in one way or another, the typical sophisticated — or, as we may call him, "standard" — storyteller develops it with conscious assiduity to the end. He explains the why as well as the how of every move; he examines the minds of his characters; he disposes his episodes so as to lead up to a crucial turning point and then gradually away from this to end on a note of finality and repose. There are many variations of the method, but such is the procedure of dozens, scores, hundreds, nay, thousands of stories, historical and invented, some in verse, some in prose.

The main model for the prose narratives was certainly the preliterate lays and epics, but there is presumably a good deal of significance in the fact that most of the standard authors of history and fiction in prose, beginning in ancient times, have been schooled in the art of composition under teachers of the "Ciceronian" tradition. The Athenian historians were schooled in rhetoric by Cicero's Greek forerunners, and the Romans and moderns mainly by Cicero himself.

Epic poetry undoubtedly supplied the model of what a story should be in its general *raison d'être*, its broad outlines, and to some extent its style; but prose is not verse, and the pioneers of the art that shines in Gibbon or Macaulay, Jane Austen or Thomas Hardy, must have learned to think consciously about prose as prose mainly in their study of the art of oratory. Not only was this the only art of composition taught in the schools, but by comparison with the deliberative oration as a form, there can have been little to invite a storyteller's emulation in any other known form of prose discourse. The other forms that lay to hand were quite unsuitable: the occasional oration wanted the momentum and tight organization that a good story (according to the example of the epics) needs; the diplomatic epistle wanted flexibility; and "prophetic" discourse was all but unknown it seems – unless we except brief oracles – among the rational-minded Greeks until imported from Jewish and Christian sources long after the art of history was perfected by Herodotus and Thucydides. But the point hardly needs arguing.

However we estimate the relative weight of the epic tradition and that of Ciceronian rhetoric as influences on the art of narration in prose, we must allow generously for the more elusive factor of nature. Epic poetry, as all students of it agree, long antedates the written versions of the Homeric poems that were read by the Athenians, and the chances are that the motives of mind and heart that have attracted men to these poems in classical and later times were the same as those that challenged the workmanship of the prehistoric bards. But what motives? I cannot see but what they were much the same as those that make one hang on the words of a great pleader for his assent at a political rally or in a legislative assembly or court of law.

For what is a story if not a "case"? It differs from a case at law or the case for or against a legislative proposal only in that its purport cannot be stated in quite such brief and forthright terms. But the difference is not so wide as might be thought. On the one hand, the storyteller often, as we have remarked, not only announces his theme explicitly at the beginning but also concludes with a compact judgement or summary of it. One thinks of Hardy's observation near the end of *Tess of the d'Urbervilles* that "the President of the Immortals had ended his sport with" her, and of the Ancient Mariner's admonition to the Wedding-Guest, "He prayeth well who loveth well / Both man and bird and beast." And on the other hand, though the debater regularly states his case in a succinct proposition, his statement is no equivalent of his whole argument — no distillation of its whole substance or force — any more than a storyteller's summary is of his story. What counts in each is not the summary but the whole "case." Something like this is true even of the summary formulas developed by mathematicians and physicists for the use of engineers, for the engineer (as opposed to the mere technician) needs to understand the meaning of the formulas as well as know the mechanics of their application.

In the next chapter we shall glance at an essentially "expository" narrative style. Our present concern is simply to urge the similarity of "standard" classical and modern narrative prose to that of deliberative argument — the kind in which Herodotus and Thucydides showed the way. The Hebrews gave us of the Western Hemisphere our religion and much that is of force in our resources of expression in language; but they had no form of discourse to teach us that could begin to rival Greek prose for the range and flexibility called for by the secular purposes of our civilization. The Hebrew mythology is unsurpassed in its kind, but it supplies no model for the occidental kind of historiography or fiction. The Greek historians and orators and their Roman imitators are the models to whom the modern storyteller — historian or novelist, reasoner, organizer, and moralist that he is — turns as by instinct.

I shall conclude this chapter with three quotations: one from Demosthenes's First Olynthiac oration urging upon the Athenian assembly the policy of supporting the city of Olynthus, threatened by Philip of Macedon; one from Thucydides's *History* that tells of the revolt of Euboea in 411 B.C.; and one from George Eliot's novel *Middlemarch*. Notice in each the energy with which the writer has probed and the urgency with which he sets forth a complex of forces which in the oration are the ground of a deliberative plea (succor must be sent to Olynthus) and in the historian and the novelist also would be precisely that if we can imagine the reader getting ready in each case to vote on the question whether he agrees or disagrees with the writer's interpretation of an important event. The orator makes use of a good deal of narrative (he recalls Philip's devastating aggressions that have preceded the present threat to Olynthus); and the narrative writers argue and moralize (Thucydides is at pains to persuade us that the despondency of the Athenians was no irrational lapse but the inevitable result of a real threat to "the whole Athenian empire" and that at the same time there were equally real grounds for hope for the Athenians in the slack character of the enemy; George Eliot, that Bulstrode acted from understandable, even if unpraiseworthy, motives in preparing to leave Middlemarch).

Demosthenes: Succor Must Be Sent to Olynthus (349 B.C.)

I believe, men of Athens, you would give much to know what is the true policy to be adopted in the present matter of inquiry. This being the case, you should be willing to hear with attention those who offer you their counsel. Besides that you will have the benefit of all preconsidered advice, I esteem it part of your good fortune that many fit suggestions will occur to some speakers at the moment, so that from them all you may easily choose what is profitable.

The present juncture, Athenians, all but proclaims aloud that you must yourselves take these affairs in hand, if you care for their success. I know not how we seem disposed in the matter. My own opinion is, vote succor immediately, and make the speediest preparations for sending it off from Athens, that you may not incur the same mishap as before; send also ambassadors to announce this, and watch the proceedings. For the danger is that this man, being unscrupulous and clever at turning events to account, making concessions when it suits him, threatening at other times (his threats may well be believed), slandering us and urging our absence against us, may convert and wrest to his use some of our main resources. Though, strange to say, Athenians, the very cause of Philip's strength is a circumstance favorable to you. His having it in his sole power to publish or conceal his designs, his being at the same time general, sovereign, paymaster, and everywhere accompanying his army, is a great advantage for quick and timely operations in war; but, for a peace with the Olynthians, which he would gladly make, it has a contrary effect. For it is plain to the Olynthians that now they are fighting, not for glory or a slice of territory, but to save their country from destruction and servitude. They know how he treated those Amphipolitans who surrendered to him their city, and those Pydneans who gave him admittance. And generally, I believe, a despotic power is mistrusted by free states, especially if their dominions are adjoining. All this being known to you, Athenians, all else of importance considered, I say, you must take heart and spirit, and apply yourselves more than ever to the war, contributing promptly, serving personally, leaving nothing undone. No plea or pretence is left you for declining your duty. What you were all so clamorous about that the Olynthians should be pressed into a war with Philip, has, of itself, come to pass, and in a way most advantageous to you. For, had they undertaken the war at your instance, they might have been slippery allies, with minds but half resolved, perhaps: but since they hate him on a quarrel of their own, their enmity is like to endure on account of their fears and their wrongs. You must not then, Athenians, forego this lucky opportunity, nor commit the error which you have often done heretofore. For example, when we returned from succoring the Euboeans, and Hierax and Stratocles of Amphipolis came to this platform, urging us to sail and receive possession of their city, if we had shown the same zeal for ourselves as for the safety of Euboea, you would have held Amphipolis then and been rid of all the troubles that ensued. Again, when news came that Pydna, Potidaea, Methone, Pagasae, and the other places (not to waste time in enumerating them) were besieged, had we to any one of these in the first instance carried prompt and reasonable succor, we should have found Philip far more tractable and humble now. But, by always neglecting the present, and imagining the future would shift for itself, we, O men of Athens, have exalted Philip, and made him greater than any king of Macedon ever was. Here, then, is come a crisis, this of Olynthus, self-offered to the state, inferior to none of the former. And, methinks, men of Athens, any man fairly estimating what the gods have done for us, notwithstanding many untoward circumstances, might with reason be grateful to them. Our numerous losses in war may justly be charged to our own negligence; but that they happened not long ago, and that an alliance, to counterbalance them, is open to our acceptance, I must regard as manifestations of divine favor. It is much the same as in money matters. If a man keep what he gets, he is thankful to fortune; if he lose it by imprudence, he loses withal his memory of the obligation. So in political affairs, they who misuse their opportunities forget even the good which the gods send them; for every prior event is judged commonly by the last result. Wherefore, Athenians, we must be exceedingly careful of our future measures, that by amendment therein we may efface the shame of the past. Should we abandon these men [the Olynthian ambassadors], too, and Philip reduce Olynthus, let any one tell me, what is to prevent him marching where he pleases? Does any one of you, Athenians, compute or consider the means by which Philip, originally weak, has become great? Having first taken Amphipolis, then Pydna, Potidaea next, Methone afterward, he invaded Thessaly. Having ordered matters at Pherae, Pagasae, Magnesia, everywhere exactly as he pleased, he departed for Thrace; where, after displacing some kings and establishing others, he fell sick; again recovering, he lapsed not into indolence, but instantly attacked the Olynthians. I omit his expeditions to Illyria and Paeonia, that against Arymbas, and some others.

Why, it may be said, do you mention all this now? That you, Athenians, may feel and understand both the folly of continually abandoning one thing after another, and the activity which forms part of Philip's habit and existence, which makes it impossible for him to rest content with his achievements. If it be his principle, ever to do more than he has done, and yours to apply yourselves vigorously to nothing, see what the end promises to be . . .[25]

Thucydides: The Revolt of Euboea (411 B.C.)

The Peloponnesians, after taking twenty-two Athenian ships, and killing or making prisoners of the crews, set up a trophy, and not long afterwards effected the revolt of the whole of Euboea (except Oreus, which was held by the Athenians themselves), and made a general settlement of the affairs of the island.

When the news of what had happened in Euboea reached Athens a panic ensued such as they had never before known. Neither the disaster in Sicily, great as it seemed at the time, nor any other had ever so much alarmed them. The camp at Samos was in revolt; they had no more ships or men to man them; they were at discord among themselves and might at any moment come to blows; and a disaster of this magnitude coming on the top of all, by which they lost their fleet, and worst of all Euboea, which was of more value to them than Attica, could not occur without throwing them into the deepest despondency. Meanwhile their greatest and most immediate trouble was the possibility that the enemy, emboldened by his victory, might make straight for them and sail against Piraeus, which they had no longer ships to defend; and every moment they expected him to arrive. This, with a little more courage, he might easily have done, in which case he would either have increased the dissensions of the city by his presence, or if he had stayed to besiege it have compelled the fleet from Ionia, although the enemy of the oligarchy, to come to the rescue of their country and of their relatives, and in the meantime would have become master of the Hellespont, Ionia, the islands, and of everything as far as Euboea, or, to speak roundly, of the whole Athenian empire. But here, as on so many other occasions, the Lacedaemonians proved the most convenient people in the world for the Athenians to be at war with. The wide difference between the two characters, the slowness and want of energy of the Lacedaemonians as contrasted with the dash and enterprise of their opponents, proved of the greatest service, especially to a maritime empire like Athens. Indeed this was shown by the Syracusans, who were most like the Athenians in character, and also most successful in combating them.

Nevertheless, upon receipt of the news, the Athenians manned twenty ships and called immediately a first assembly in the Pnyx, where they had been used to meet formerly, and deposed the Four Hundred and voted to hand over the government to the Five Thousand, of which body all who furnished a suit of armor were to be members, decreeing also that no one should receive pay for the discharge of any office, or if he did should be held accursed . . .[26]

George Eliot: Bulstrode Decides to Leave Middlemarch

Who can know how much of his most inward life is made up of the thoughts he believes other men to have about him, until that fabric of opinion is threatened with ruin?

Bulstrode was only the more conscious that there was a deposit of uneasy presentiment in his wife's mind, because she carefully avoided any allusion to it. He had been used every day to taste the flavor of supremacy and the tribute of complete deference; and the certainty that he was watched or measured with a hidden suspicion of his having some discreditable secret, made his voice totter when he was speaking to edification. Foreseeing, to men of Bulstrode's anxious temperament, is often worse than seeing; and his imagination continually heightened the anguish of an imminent disgrace. Yes, imminent; for if his defiance of Raffles did not keep the man away — and though he prayed for this result he hardly hoped for it — the disgrace was certain. In vain he said to himself that, if permitted, it would be a divine visitation, a chastisement, a preparation; he recoiled from the imagined burning; and he judged that it must be more for the Divine glory that he should escape dishonor. That recoil had at last urged him to make preparations for quitting Middlemarch. If evil truth must be reported of him, he would then be at a less scorching distance from the contempt of his old neighbors; and in a new scene, where his life would not have gathered the same wide sensibility, the tormentor, if he pursued him, would be less formidable. To leave the place finally would, he knew, be extremely painful to his wife, and on other grounds he would have preferred to stay where he had struck root. Hence he made his preparations at first in a conditional way, wishing to leave on all sides an opening for his return after brief absence, if any favorable intervention of Providence should dissipate his fears. He was preparing to transfer his management of the Bank, and to give up any active control of other commercial affairs in the neighborhood, on the ground of his failing health, but without excluding his future resumption of such work. The measure would cause him some added expense and some diminution of income beyond what he had already undergone from the general depression of trade; and the Hospital presented itself as a principal object of outlay on which he could fairly economize.

This was the experience which had determined his conversation with Lydgate. . . .[27]

THE EXPOSITORY STYLE

Treatise · Lesson · Sermon

Clown. Give me leave. Here lies the water; good. Here stands the man; good. If the man go to this water and drown himself, it is, will he, nill he, he goes, — mark you that? But if the water come to him and drown him, he drowns not himself; argal, he that is not guilty of his own death shortens not his own life. — *Hamlet*, V, i, 16–22

W E SATISFY our curiosity about anything if we are able to say that it is or does, preferably is, such and such.[1] If it moves, we like to state the idea by saying that it is mobile or is capable of motion. To say this is to stop its motion and make it static. We comprehend it by holding it still and equating it with something else. If we say that a boat is mobile, we are identifying the boat with all things mobile.

I would argue that an expository statement is typically an equation ("A is B"; "mice are mammals"). By *typically* I mean not that simple, outwardly balanced equations like "mice are mammals" necessarily make up a large proportion of any expository work but that the aim or ideal of exposition is everywhere to approximate such simple, categorical propositions. They are actually rather few and far between in most treatises, but they are nuggets of truth in which the mind takes peculiar satisfaction. They are the home runs that one would like to make every time at bat. We like to find a true, fixed relation between one thing and something else, and to be able to state it in the form "subject is (or equals) predicate-noun or predicate-adjective," with luck finding for our subject and predicate words whose similar form will enforce the equivalence expressed by the copula. It will be noticed, too, in many expository pieces, especially in the stricter sciences, that things or ideas belonging to a given classification are often designated by words having some common element, by which, when the things are named as a series, their relation is more or less represented to the eye or ear, as with chemical compounds of a given class or the cases of Latin nouns.

Good expository prose is coherent: sentence members of like grammatical order, and groups of sentences, are often linked together by similarities of form, repeated key words, and the like, but, except where concerned to present a tightly reasoned argument (e.g., a theorem in plane geometry), commonly diffusive rather than closely unified. Even in the presentation of scientific theorems there is usually nothing in the outward features of the prose to emphasize the drawing together of the whole at the end into a striking conclusion. The logic may be strict and the conclusion impressive, even exciting, to the well-qualified reader, but the style may be bare and monotonous throughout.

A description of such an object as a machine or a zoological specimen or the analysis of a biblical text, as in a doctrinal sermon, or any section of such a description or analysis, will ordinarily begin with a topic sentence, and the rest will consist of explanations of the terms or implications of this sentence — restatements, illustrations, comparisons, and contrasts. Any one of these extensions of the topic sentence may run to any length. A typical piece may therefore be said to have a beginning and a middle, but no logically predetermined end.

The following passages will serve to illustrate some, at least, of the foregoing observations.

Six cases are commonly distinguished in Latin nouns: nominative, genitive, dative, accusative, ablative, and vocative.

Indirect quotation or indirect discourse occurs most frequently after verbs of saying, thinking, knowing, and the like.

But if the middle be universal in respect to either extreme, when universal belongs to the major either affirmatively or negatively, but to the minor particularly, and in a manner opposite to the universal, (I mean by opposition, if the universal be negative, but the particular affirmative, or if the universal is affirmative, but the particular negative,) it is necessary that a particular negative syllogism should result. For if M is present with no N, but with a certain O, N must necessarily not be present with a certain O, for since a negative proposition is convertible, N will be present with no M, but M was by hypothesis present with a certain O, wherefore N will not be present with a certain O, for a syllogism is produced in the first figure.[2]

Cell-walls may become modified by the impregnation of various substances. Woody or lignified cell-walls appear to contain substances called *coniferin* and *vanillin*, in addition to various other compounds which are imperfectly known. Lignified tissues are colored yellow by aniline sulphate or aniline chloride, violet with phloroglucin and hydrochloric acid, and characteristic reactions are also given by mixtures containing phenol, indol, skatol, thallin, sulphate, &c. . . . Staining reagents can also be used to differentiate lignified cell-walls. Cuticularized or suberized cell-walls occur especially in those cells which perform a protective function. They are impervious to water and gases. Both cuticularized or suberized membranes are insoluble in cuprammonia, and are colored yellow or brown in a solution of chlor-iodide of zinc. It is probable that the corky or suberized cells do not contain any cellulose . . .; whilst cuticularized cells are only modified in their outer layers, cellulose inner layers being still recognizable. The suberized and cuticularized cell-walls appear to contain a fatty body called suberin, and such cell-walls can be stained red by a solution of alcanin, the lignified and cellulose membranes remaining unstained.[3]

In exposition like this there is no need for climactic or carefully timed effects, and, as already intimated in the last chapter, the reader of a treatise loses nothing essential if interrupted, but may, indeed, with advantage vary the speed of his reading, pause to reflect upon a detail here and there, or lay the text aside altogether and make a fresh start after an interval of rest. Timing and incremental effects are important in expository prose only to lecturers or preachers, whose object is something more than mere exposition. A lecture or sermon, though its substance be instruction, is instruction that needs to be driven home within a fixed span of minutes to a present audience subject to fatigue, and therefore requires the speaker to make use of some of the same devices that mark deliberative eloquence. Deliberative discourse is typically spoken; but exposition is typically written, for its substance is not, like that of a deliberative plea, something shaped for a single occasion, but a truth unaffected by the passage of time, and often one that is too complex to be fully assimilated by an addressee at a single hearing. It is significant that lecturers often utilize blackboards and other exhibits, and that lectures are often (but political speeches seldom) given in series.

But such eloquence as we find in sermons and lectures is not quite the same thing as that in a parliamentary speech. The primary aim of the deliberative speaker is in the effect of his words here and now, not in supplying matter for his audience to take home for contemplation or future reference. But it is normally the main concern of the preacher or lecturer that his message be remembered, and his eloquence will often be in the way of persistent repetition and restatement rather than in reasoned argumentation. I believe I am right in saying that a sermon can usually be trimmed to order more or less casually, whereas any contemplated lengthening or shortening of a deliberative oration is likely to require revision of its entire internal organization.

Needless to say, political orators often preach, and preachers often argue, and opinions may properly differ as to whether the virtue of a sober, rational deliberative plea be mainly that of good philosophy or good rhetoric, or, in other terms, whether the force of the rhetoric be that of eloquence or merely that of good exposition.

It is natural to look to the literature of science for the most purely expository style — the style least influenced by the tactics of deliberative argument — but science is a big word, and the style of many a treatise whose title, taken alone, might seem to announce a work of cool exposition, like Darwin's *The Origin of Species* or Sir Charles Lyell's *Principles of Geology* (1830–33), is as carefully organized to anticipate and overcome popular opposition as if the subject had been avowedly, as it was actually in each case, not only controversial but controversial because of its human and not merely scientific bearings. In these works all of the graces of tactful persuasion are to be seen: the writer's care to raise the kind of questions that would occur to readers unversed in the subject ("How will the struggle for existence . . . act in regard to variation? Can the principle of selection, which we have seen is so potent in the hands of man, apply under nature?"), exhortation ("Let the endless number of slight variations . . . in our domestic productions . . . be borne in mind . . . Let it also be borne in mind how infinitely complex . . . are the mutual relations of all organic beings . . ."),[4] exclamation, forward and backward cross-reference, a good deal of distinctly literatesque phrasing first and last ("I know not";[5] "How fleeting are the wishes and efforts of man! How short his time"),[6] and the careful placing of arguments with regard to the principle of climax ("Lastly, and this I am inclined to think is the most important element, a dominant species . . . &c.").[7]

Still, the distinction between exposition and pleading, especially between scientific or technical and deliberative argument, is both sound and important. I believe it is true to say that the master of the popular debater's art is seldom the master scientist, or vice versa. In the long story of what Andrew D. White called "the warfare of science with theology in Christendom," at least down to the twentieth century, popular eloquence has more often been turned against than in favor of scientific innovations; and the scientists, whose exacting labors have never afforded them much opportunity for practice in popular apologetics, and indeed whose way of thinking practically necessitates their remaining indifferent to popular opinion, have labored under a heavy handicap. Today so complete is the revolution that has taken place, and within living memory, that not only has a prevailing reverence for science replaced the old suspicion; it has had the corrupting effect of encouraging all manner of quackery to borrow the prestige of authentic science by masquerading under its honorable name. On this point nothing could be more revealing than the unneeded terminology got up to look technical that disfigures the prose written by professors of several of the modern pseudosciences.

The mischief is pretentiousness: the attempt to impose conviction by means of a mode of expression traditionally associated with irresistible authority. The mode today is pseudo-technical terminology; in the first century of modern England it was balanced construction and a parade of learned allusions and images drawn from what is commonly known as the old "unnatural natural history" and other old-fashioned sciences.

The Elizabethan pretension was didactic rather than cabalistic. The modern quack aims to mystify laymen with professional abracadabra; the Elizabethan to instruct. What the Elizabethan delighted to teach was science, if by science we understand a more bookish and inclusive sense of the word than it bears today; and though the old science or sciences most influential on prose style were not abreast of the newest discoveries of their time, they were by and large respectable in educated eyes, because traditional. But the Elizabethan affectation of a scientific-didactic style for more or less all purposes was not, like the affectation of jargon in our time, confined to quacks and a limited—even if large—circle of naïve, half-educated followers; rather it was a universally diffused habit of mind, a legacy of the dogmatic character of medieval philosophy. The typical teacher in the old tradition was the kind who laid down the law, not the kind who encouraged speculation or experiment; and his style of expression was that to which the present chapter is devoted, only more so, if the expression may be allowed: that is, a style in which the perfectly, even elaborately, balanced categorical predication is the favorite expression, and in which series of parallel words and constructions are conspicuous.

The Elizabethan Age is known by tradition as the golden age of the English Renaissance, and the commonest meaning of the word "Renaissance" is a rebirth of European culture from the seed of humanism. The traditional view makes much of the Ciceronians, the Platonists, and the historiographers; and we hear much also concerning the playwrights who imitated classical models; but there are wide areas in the history of ideas and in the history of prose style that the revival of classical studies does little to explain.

The Tudor Age was by no means one of great parliamentary activity or great deliberative expression. The Ciceronian influence was never so strong in England as on the Continent and in England during the sixteenth century hardly extended outside the limited circle of scholars writing in Latin. In vernacular literature it may be allowed to have had something to do with the careful organization of Sidney's near-great political prose-epic, *Arcadia,* and it certainly furnished both the form and the style of his *Defense of Poesie,* as it did also the form and style of Hooker's defense of the Anglican Church. But these writings are exceptions. A few Elizabethans were rough-and-ready journalists (as we shall notice in the fifth chapter), and Bacon, in the *Essays,* in a sense we shall presently consider, was a prophet. But it would not be far from the truth to assert that Elizabeth's subjects taken together, including even Ciceronians, journalists, and prophets, to say nothing of scriveners, were, by tradition if not by instinct, teachers and preachers — prosers one and all — rather than champions of the only cause that has ever inspired supreme eloquence — political freedom. When the Elizabethan speaks to us in prose, it is generally as if he were looking at us over a pair of spectacles and holding a ferule in his hand.

The prevailing style of his prose is euphuism, a style that long antedated Lyly's novel, as is now well known. Croll has shown how conspicuous the euphuistic features (especially parison, paromoion, and isocolon) are in typical Latin treatises of the Middle Ages, and is certainly right in arguing that euphuism by no means originated, as scholars once thought, under classical influence, but rather represents a mere perpetuation in the English vernacular of the over-schematized (ultimately Alexandrian, therefore postclassical) style of exposition common in monkish Latin.[8]

For euphuism is only a name for a somewhat exaggerated pointing up, under the influence of rhetoricians of the Second Sophistic tradition, of the essential features of a generic style that can be identified in strict expository prose everywhere and at all times: in Aristotle as well as in Bede or Thomas à Kempis or John Lyly; in Euclid, Pliny the Elder, Machiavelli, Descartes, Newton, Kant, Darwin, Matthew Arnold, Karl Marx — in short, in the work of every strict philosopher, scientist, or doctrinal preacher since the world began. Nor is there any logical way of saying where the line is to be drawn between the generic style in its irreducible features and the ornamented variety. The requirements of strict exposition inevitably lead not only to a certain amount of balance and parallelism, but also, given a subject matter of any complexity, to the emphatic marking of the correspondences of ideas by correspondences of form indistinguishable, merely as form, from the most elaborate affectations of the euphuist. The rule could be stated, of course, that correspondences of form should not be exploited beyond what clarity or perspicuity or mnemonic convenience calls for, but opinions could differ widely as to its application. Cicero himself recognized the inevitably "euphuistic" character of sober expository prose, and Quintilian remarks that the style between the "grand" (ἁδρόν) and the "plain" (ἰσχνόν) is known indifferently as the "medium" and the "floridum" (ἀνθηρόν).[9]

The "genus medium" is a "genus" identified by predecessors of Cicero as a vague something-or-other between the "genus humile" and the "genus grande."[10] Cicero and Quintilian find the "genus modicum" or "mediocre" mainly fitted for the office of "pleasing" ("modicum in delectando"), and emphasize its "soothing" or "suave" or "flowing" character, in contrast to what they see as the exciting quality of the "grande." In it "all the charms of language and thought are intertwined."[11] The thing that first called attention to the distinct identity of this style was probably not scientific or philosophical prose but highly euphuistic oratory of the epideictic sort, but Cicero recognized the generic identity of the two things, and some of his observations about them are most illuminating.

Epideictic speeches, says Cicero, "were produced as show pieces"; they comprise "eulogies, descriptions, histories, and exhortations . . . and all other speeches unconnected with battles of public life." The speaker "indulges in a neatness and symmetry of sentences"; in the ornamentation there is "no attempt at concealment . . . so that words correspond to words as if measured off in equal phrases; frequently things opposed are placed side by side and things contrasted are paired; clauses are made to end in the same way with similar sound." And Cicero remarks the difference between this style and the deliberative when he says that it is "spurned and rejected in the forum" and little heard in legal practice. Local outward patterning of word groups is conspicuous and incurs the reproach that the prose often suggests "verselets and is often over-ornamented." [12]

Cicero's recognition of the generic identity of this ornate epideictic style and the style characteristically written by the philosophers is clear and assured. His remarks strike the modern reader at first as extremely queer. One would expect him to explain that the convenience of symmetrical patterning for the communication of scientific or philosophical ideas would account for its appearance in the prose of a Plato or an Aristotle — that is, its convenience for purposes of logical economy, clarity, and perspicuity — but instead Cicero speaks as if the philosophers, among whom he specifically includes Aristotle and Plato *in this context*, borrowed the style from the epideictic orators and cultivated it primarily for the pleasure it affords the ear.[13] The philosophers, he says, "talk with scholars, whose minds they prefer to soothe rather than arouse; they talk in this way about unexciting and non-controversial subjects, and for the purpose of instructing rather than persuading ("docendi causa, non capiendi locuntur"); [14] and again, "not so much to persuade as to delight" ("nec tam persuadere quam delectare").[15] In distinguishing the functions of the three "genera dicendi," he says that that of the middle "genus" is to give pleasure ("quot officia oratoris, tot . . . genera dicendi . . . modicum in delectando").[16] In this style there is "a minimum of vigor and a maximum of charm" ("nervorum . . . minimum, suavitatis . . . autem plurimum").[17] He goes on to repeat that it is out of the philosophic schools that orators who speak in this style come and, more specifically, remarks that "The sophists [by which word he can only be referring to representatives of the *Second* Sophistic school] are the source from which all this has flowed into the forum." [18]

I have quoted these remarks at length as ideal testimony to the formal identity of the prose of strict exposition with the euphuistic prose of occasional oratory. The notion of Plato or Aristotle writing on "non-controversial" issues, and for the purpose of "soothing" or "pleasing" rather than "persuading" the reader (and notice the close association in his mind between instruction and "suavitas" — how many schoolboys would agree with him?), is enough to make one stare; but the correctness of Cicero's observation of the thing he is trying to explain is placed beyond the shadow of a doubt by the impossible explanation it forced him to invent. And let us not overlook, in passing, the interesting light thus thrown on the way of thinking of this supreme specialist in the art of eloquence. One would not belittle his quality or influence in the realm of ideas, but the home of his mind was not the schools of philosophy but the law courts and the senate, where the spoken word decided success or failure, so that it became second nature for him to reason from words to ideas instead of the other way around. The truth is doubtless equally accessible or difficult of access by either route, but there is no doubt that when rhetoricians go wrong it is commonly because of their too little respect for ideas as such (witness the bad name earned by the whole tribe of the Alexandrian sophists), just as when philosophers go wrong it is often through too little respect for the art of rhetoric. Some of the ancient Stoics were damned already by their contemporaries for their obscurity;[19] and no complaint is more often heard in American universities today from scientists themselves than that their students and not a few of their colleagues are unable to express themselves in writing with accuracy, let alone elegance.

The neutral element in most expository prose is, of course, enormous, as I am reminded on looking over these expository pages of my own. My propositions are equations often enough to be seen as characteristic (as in the preceding and the present sentences: "element . . . is . . . enormous," "propositions are equations"); and, when so, fairly often exhibit one or more schemata that point up the equivalence of the things equated (alliteration in "element . . . enormous"; homeoteleuton in "propositions . . . equations"); but "Stilistik," needless to say, is not one of the exacter sciences, and would look ridiculous in euphuistic dress.

The typical scientific statement is firm and forthright, I had almost said categorical. It may be limited by a conditional clause or other restrictive expression, but, other than stated restrictions, there will be no ifs or buts — no implied imponderables or variables — to be allowed for. Scientific "truths" have a way of going out of date and being replaced by newer ones, but their usefulness while they last depends upon their strictness, which corresponds to the familiar traditional assumption that nature's processes are perfectly regular.

No wonder, then, if we think of the impressive achievements of science, that the moralist, whether in church, Hyde Park, or other place where people gather to hear occasional sermonizing, religious or secular, eulogies, obituaries, and the like, should want to wear the same air of authority that is implicit in the style in which science lays down its awesome law. Not that preachers are necessarily imitating the scientists; rather that both find schematized expression the most strongly suggestive of the foursquare authority of whatever it is employed to state. Given examples of schematized moralistic prose may or may not be thought to be in good taste; one speaker in this vein may strike us as impertinent, another as sublime. Any collection of sermons will show that the vein is perennial in the pulpit. I have before me such a collection, and in the first paragraph of the first page I find this sentence: "Another man sees an engine in the kettle, a new language in the clouds, an angel in the marble, a hero in the child, a people in the multitude, and he becomes an inventor, an artist, a prophet, a statesman." [20] On the third page I find: "His eye was single, and He was full of light. He saw things whole and He saw things clear." [21] In the same sermon in the fourth paragraph from the end, seven sentences in a row begin with the pronoun "you," and all but the first with the words, "you can not." [22] I could fill many pages with like references, as any churchgoer will allow, for I don't suppose I have ever heard a sermon that did not exhibit more or less of such schematizing.

In the introductory chapter I referred in passing to the schematic prose that we find off and on and, as it were, by accident in such documents as logbooks and records like the *Anglo-Saxon Chronicle*. It is of trifling, indeed all but negligible, significance, but for the sake of completeness I should illustrate what I have in mind. It is simply that entries in series reporting one kind of matter tend to fall into one and the same form of expression. Thus in the *Anglo-Saxon Chronicle* many entries in a row (whether or not skipping one or

more blank years) may begin with "Her" ("here") or "Her on
þys[s] [um] geare" or "On þis gear," and the variety of the events
recorded will be very limited, so that those of only one or two kinds
may be the first set down under several consecutive years. Here are
the beginnings of the entries for several years in the E manuscript
(dots represent my omissions):

997. Her þissum geare ferde se here abutan Defnanscire into
Saefernmuoan . . .

998. Her wende se here eft eastweard into Frommuðan . . .

999. Her com se here eft abuton into Temese, ond wendon þa
up andlang Medewaegan to Hrofeceastre . . .

1000. Her on þissum geare se cyng ferde into Cumerlande . . .

1001. Her com se here to Exanmuðan, ond up ða eodon to ðaere
byrig . . .

1002. Her on þissum geare se cyng geraedde on his witan, þaet
man sceolde gafol gyldan þam flotan ond frið wið hi niman . . .

1003. Her waes Exacester abrocen þurh þone Frenciscan ceorl
Hugon . . .

1004. Her com Swegen mid his flotan to Norowic . . .

1005. Her on þyssum geare waes se mycla hungor geond An-
gelcynn . . .[23]

And of course this kind of schematization is precisely what we
find in those chapters of the Old Testament that recount genealogies,
successions of kings, and divisions of property (see for example
Genesis xxxvi; most of I Chronicles; Ezra ii; etc., etc.).

If I had to name one worst and one best example of prose schematized for homiletic purposes in English, I should pick respectively
Lyly's *Euphues* and Lincoln's Gettysburg Address; and for a good
standard style for the workaday expository writer to emulate, what
could be better than that of the Queen Anne journalists?

The badness of *Euphues* is not only that its schematization is
fantastically elaborate and persistent, but that whether seen as scientific-didactic or as homiletic discourse it is monstrously inappropri-
ate to a work of fiction, even of fiction meant for edification. Those
Elizabethans who put pen to paper, almost to a man, were, as I
have remarked, relentless prosers, no matter what genre they were
writing in, and their schoolmasterish habits bespeak a prevailing
smugness. It is difficult to imagine any other age producing a John

Lyly or reading *Euphues* with patience, much less idolizing and imitating it, as the Elizabethans did for ten or fifteen years. The laboriously over-schematized style that it made fashionable is tedious enough in a work properly didactic, like Ascham's *Scholemaster* or *Toxophilus*, but positively insulting in a novel. A jilted lover who could speak the following words without facetious or ironical intent — and this lover, as the context shows, is wholly serious — corresponds to nothing on earth or in the imagination:

I haue loued you long, and now at the length [I] must leaue you, whose harde heart I will not impute to discurtesie, but destinie, it contenteth me that I dyed in fayth, though I coulde not liue in fauour, neyther was I euer more desirous to begin my loue, then I am now to ende my life. Thinges which cannot be altered are to be borne, not blamed: follies past are sooner remembred then redressed, and time lost may well be repented, but neuer recalled. I will not recount the passions I haue suffered, I think the effect show them, and now it is more behoo[ue]full for me to fall to praying for a new life, then to remember the olde: yet this I ad [de] (which though it merit no mercy to saue, it deserueth thankes of a friend) that onely I loued thee, and liued for thee, and howe dye for thee. And so turning on my left side, I fetched a deepe sigh.[24]

People have sometimes spoken of euphuism as "flowery," a word half suggesting that its ornaments, including images, are meant to have the flavor of poetry. "Poetical" images occur in some prose that is otherwise euphuistic, but the characteristic images of Lyly, and of his imitators too for the most part, are drawn, like the schemata and the whole way of thinking, from science or philosophy, and they find their most characteristic expression not in the subtle way of metaphor but in the more analytical, explicit way of simile or literal comparison. In the following passage the only metaphors are "smokie" and "shadows," which, however, are of the well-crystallized variety, all the other objects of reference being not really images at all, strictly speaking, since they do not occur in figures but only in literal propositions:

They that vse to steale Honny burne Hemlocke to smoke the Bees from their hiues, and it may bee, that to get some aduauntage of me, you haue vsed these smokie arguments, thinking thereby to smother me with the conceipt of strong imagination. But as the

Camelion though he haue most guttes draweth least breath, or as the Elder tree though hee bee fullest of pith, is farthest from strength: so though your resons seeme inwardly to your selfe somewhat substantiall, and your perswasions pithie in your owne conceipte, yet beeing well wayed without, they be shadows without substaunce, and weake without force.[25]

The Gettysburg Address is a lay sermon, but invokes religion both explicitly and implicitly. The opening sentence (a narrative statement) is something like a text, which the speaker then goes on to analyze (its diction is biblical: "four score and seven," "our fathers"). Then comes a bit of more topical narrative ("Now we are engaged in a great civil war . . ."); then an argument (on the theme "It is for us the living, rather, to be dedicated here . . ."), concluding with the famous phrase "government of the people, by the people, for the people," which recalls the opening sentence. The whole moves climactically as to the relative force of the several ideas presented, but it is an exhortation and not an argument, the logical, argumentative part being only incidental. The structure is loose compared with that of a logical argument; but a fine coherence is secured by means of the schemata (e.g., "we are engaged . . . We are met . . . We have come"; "The world will little note, nor long remember"; etc., etc.) and by the repetition here and there of words like "nation" and "dedicate"; and the climactic order of the ideas is enforced by half-concealed changes of meaning in one of the repeated words, the first personal pronoun, which now stands for the speaker and his colleagues on the platform, now for them and the assembled people, now for the whole population of the country, and at least once for the whole human race ("us the living").

Four score and seven years ago our fathers brought forth on this continent, a new nation, conceived in Liberty, and dedicated to the proposition that all men are created equal.

Now we are engaged in a great civil war, testing whether that nation, or any nation so conceived and so dedicated, can long endure. We are met on a great battle-field of that war. We have come to dedicate a portion of that field, as a final resting place for those who here gave their lives that that nation might live. It is altogether fitting and proper that we should do this.

But, in a larger sense, we cannot dedicate — we can not consecrate — we can not hallow — this ground. The brave men, living and dead, who struggled here, have consecrated it, far above our poor power to add or detract. The world will little note, nor long remember what we say here, but it can never forget what they did here. It is for us the living, rather, to be dedicated here to the unfinished work which they who fought here have thus far so nobly advanced. It is rather for us to be here dedicated to the great task remaining before us — that from these honored dead we take increased devotion to that cause for which they gave the last full measure of devotion — that we here highly resolve that these dead shall not have died in vain — that this nation, under God, shall have a new birth of freedom — and that government of the people, by the people, for the people, shall not perish from the earth.[26]

THE TUMBLING STYLE

Its Origin and Incidence

"This may wel be rym dogerel," quod he.
— Chaucer's Host of the *Canterbury Tales*

I NOW undertake to identify a type of style which, however conspicuous its earmarks, may not offhand seem definable, like the
other types I have distinguished, with reference to a particular or
primary function. I see it as a narrative style, and must therefore
meet the question whether it differs essentially from the styles I
treat as narrative counterparts of the deliberative, the expository,
and the prophetic.

It would be idle to pretend that the narrative thread or other rational substance of a tumbling piece, seen in the abstract, is in any
way distinctive, and I recognize, as I reiterate below (p. 65), that
the style turns up now and then for special effects in many a text
whose prevailing style belongs to one or another of the other cate-
gories I have defined. The reason I have felt bound to treat it as
of parallel order with these other styles is that there are texts — many,
both early and late — in which the tumbling manner, with the point
of view it implies, is so insistent and unrelenting, and its command
of the reader's attention therefore so imperious and, in a sense, so
independent of whatever other interest the piece may offer, that it
has indeed a function of its own. This function is that of poetry, as
opposed to prose.

An actual poetry was its historical source, as we shall see, and though it retained the metrical features of the parent medium only in a relaxed, intermittent, and haphazard fashion, the vestiges of meter that it did retain and its characteristic diction and imagery express an attitude toward the subject matter on the writer's part that is positively that of a poet. If it be asked wherein a poet's attitude toward his matter differs from that of a prose writer, my answer would be that in prose the characteristic assumption of both writer and reader is that the subject has an identity and an interest apart from the words, whereas in poetry it is assumed that word and idea are inseparable.

In two respects the tumbling variety of prose is comparable to the prophetic, wherein the ideas — at least the important ones — are likewise inseparable (in fact, though not in theory) from the words and the emotional appeal is often strong. But there is a difference. The appeal of the prophet is always primarily to the intellect, whereas that of the tumbling writer — in verse or in prose — with his swingeing, dynamic coil and hubbub, is much more directly to the feelings. So much so, indeed, that in many a text the writer seems hardly to care who's who or what is at stake so long as he has an excuse to unload a big, hard-hitting word-hoard. This is especially true of news reports of sporting events in the American tradition, where the story pounds its way forward in one and the same manner no matter who wins or makes the more spectacular plays or errors or shows the better or worse sportsmanship. I have put my comment in rather scornful terms, mainly, I suppose, because weary of the flood of this strident type of writing that pours from the presses daily, most of it unleavened by any spark of distinction; but there is no denying that the feature of impartiality in the gusto with which the writer treats friend and foe alike is not without its revered counterpart in the great lays and epics of the heroic age.

But we must get on with a more particular description of its features.

Of the several poetical genres of the early Germanic peoples represented in the surviving literature, the heroic narrative known as the "lay" is the only one of substantial length that seems to have been indigenous; and it will be remembered that poems of early date in Anglo-Saxon that we call "lyrics," such as "The Wanderer," "The Seafarer," and "The Far-Traveler" ("Widsiþ"), are regularly cast in narrative form. Whatever the origin of the verse form, it has been associated, time out of mind, more with narrative than with non-narrative discourse.

There is a marked difference between the effects of alliterative-accentual verse according as it runs much or little to those types of half-line in which the stressed syllables fall together (Sievers's types C, X / / X, and D_1, / / \ X, or D_2, / / X \) or in which a stressed syllable is immediately followed or preceded by a half-stressed (D_1, as noted, and E, / \ X / or / X \ /), on the one hand, and, on the other, those in which there is an alternation of stressed with unstressed syllables. Verses of the latter kind can be as undulating and sweet as those of an Elizabethan song, as in the refrain of "Deor" ("Ðaes ofereode, ðisses swa maeg"); while at the other extreme we have the muscular, thumping movement produced by the crowding of stressed and half-stressed syllables: a movement peculiarly suited to passages about the curdling or spilling of blood or the din of the mead-hall. Consider the following:

> þryð-swyð beheold
> maeʒ Hyʒelaces,   hu se man-scaða
> under faer-ʒripum   ʒefaran wolde.
> Ne þaet se aʒlaeca   yldan þohte,
> ac he ʒefenʒ hraðe   forman siðe
> slaependne rinc,   slat unwearnum,
> bat ban-locan,   blod edrum dranc,
> syn-snaedum swealh;   sona haefde
> unlyfiʒendes   eal ʒefeormod,
> fet ond folma.

(Strong and mighty, Hygelac's kinsman watched the man-scather and his fearsome grips to see what he would do. Nor did the monster think to tarry; on the contrary, his first move was quickly to snatch a sleeping warrior; he tore him to pieces without hindrance, bit his bone-locker, drank his blood in streams, and swallowed him in big gulps; soon he had devoured all of the unliving one, even the feet and hands.) [1]

Poets writing in any of the varieties of verse form that were standard from *Tottel's Miscellany* to the Romantic Revival, whether in rising or falling rhythm and in lines of whatever length, can, and do more often than the Anglo-Saxon poets, achieve the perfection of graceful, lilting music; and they can also, of course, approximate the hard-hitting, bumpy movement of the passage I have just quoted from *Beowulf* by crowding their lines with secondary stresses ("And where is that same great seven-headed beast?"; "A shout that tore hell's concave, and beyond"); but in this vein they are denied — or, if one prefer, denied themselves — the Anglo-Saxon's resource of putting two *fully* stressed syllables together *with no pause between* (exceptions could be pointed out, but they are few and negligible). This Anglo-Saxon "one-two" — to borrow a phrase from boxing — is simply inadmissible, as if the poets who standardized the modern system had met in conclave and ruled it out as too barbarously emphatic for civilized use; and it is fair to say that even the crowding of lines with secondary stresses is something that the standard poets (as opposed to late slashers like Browning) use for the most part with an eye — or ear — to special effects, whereas in Anglo-Saxon poetry the "crowded" half-lines are regular alternatives for the "uncrowded." When we confront standard modern verse with that of our pre-Conquest forebears, the characteristic forte of the modern is seen to be graceful movement and the emotions such movement is fitted to express, and that of the alliterative-accentual, *res gestae* with blades, teeth, and mead-horns.

Notice in the passage quoted from *Beowulf* the brawny theme and the gory details. Notice the hammerblows struck by the stressed, closed monosyllables "rinc," "slat," "bat," "blod," "dranc," "swealh," and "fet." Notice the bulging effect of those compound words that bump twice: "þryð-swyð," "man-scaða," "faer-ʒripum," "ban-locan," and "syn-snaedum." These make big mouthfuls. Notice that two of these are kennings — expressions which by means of metaphor explain or amplify the idea for which they stand — and notice the apparent crudity of one of them, "ban-locan" for "body" (compare "ban-hus" or "bone-house" in *Beowulf* 2508 and 3147 and in *St. Guthlac* 1341). Perhaps the idea had a meaning for the Anglo-Saxons that is lost to the modern reader, to whom, though its roundaboutness no doubt implies the virtue of energy in the poet and the alliteration with "bat" may be thought to support the idea of crack-ing bones, it seems deplorably gauche. Do we not detect here, as in many another Anglo-Saxon kenning, an uncritical delight in word-coining for its own sake, as if it were unworthy of a poet to call anything by its ordinary name? Is it not precisely the same motive as that which produces uncountable metaphors, good, bad, and in-different, for home runs, errors, touchdowns, baskets, and the like, on the sports pages of today's American newspapers?

But the comparison cannot be pressed, for the sports reporter nearly always writes in the comic spirit, and the Anglo-Saxon poet everywhere — apparently — in earnest. In the passage quoted we are clearly meant to shudder and not smile as the bones crack and the big gulps go down. Is it any wonder that the author of *Piers Plow-man*, writing in the old verse form three centuries after the Conquest, when comparisons with French poetry were inevitable, should have worn it with a difference?

For though *Piers Plowman* communicates a profoundly serious message, its thumping, pummeling lines are full of earthy humor. No English poet before the Conquest or for long thereafter let fly so many coarse words or had so much fun with them. How original this poet was in the new perspective thus implied we need not trouble to inquire; but the poem stands a convenient illustration of a rule applying generally to modern writers of the old style, whether in verse or in prose. With nearly all of them it is a half-comic pose. The more energetically they lay it on, the more clearly they let us understand that its bark is meant to be a degree worse than its bite. The new way is to match the pile-driving emphasis of the rhythm with a heightening of idea to — or toward — absurdity, as in the fol-lowing lines from *Piers Plowman*:

And þanne cam couetise   can I hym nouȝte descryue,
So hungriliche and holwe   sire Heruy hym loked.
He was bitelbrowed   and baberlipped also,
With two blered eyȝhen   as a blynde hagge;
And as a letheren purs   lolled his chekes,
Wel sydder þan his chyn   þei chiueled for elde;
And as a bondman of his bacoun   his berde was bidraueled.
With an hode on his hed   a lousi hatte aboue,

And in a tauny tabarde of twelue wynter age,
Al totorne and baudy and ful of lys crepynge;
But if þat a lous couthe haue lopen þe bettre,
She sholde nouȝte haue walked on that welche so was it
thredebare.[2]

Anglo-Saxon poetry was a strong influence on the style of Aelfric's prose sermons in the tenth century; and the alliterative-accentual school of the fourteenth century, and more particularly *Piers Plowman*, a comparable influence on the prose of the pamphlet literature that anticipated and accompanied the English Reformation. The striking features of the prose in both cases are its frequent approximation of the meter or alliteration, or both, of the poetry and its prevailingly loose sentence structure. In both cases we notice also, though not so much in Aelfric, a fondness for the swelling effect of plenty of secondarily stressed syllables. The essential difference is that Aelfric writes with restraint and the utmost seriousness, whereas the pamphleteers let go with abandon and gaiety. The fact of English prose so distinctly imitative of alliterative verse in two widely separated ages seems interesting enough to warrant illustration. Here is Aelfric:

Ðes foresaeda halga wer waes gewunod þaet he wolde gan on niht to sae ond standan on ðam sealtan brymme oð his swyran, syngende his gebedu. Ða on sumere nihte hlosnode sum oder munuc his faereldes ond mid sleaccre stalcunge his fotswaþum filigde, oðþaet hi begen to sae becomon. Ða dyde Cuðberhtus swa his gewuna waes, sang his gebedu on saelicere yðe standende oð þone swyran, ond syððan his cneowa on ðam ceosle gebigde, astrehtum handbredum to heofenlicum rodore. Efne ða comon twegen seolas of saelicum grunde, ond hi mid heora flyse his fet drygdon, ond mid heora blaede his leoma beðedon, ond siððan mid gebeacne his bletsunge baedon, licgende aet his foton on fealwum ceosle. Ða cuðberhtus þa saelican nytenu on sund asende mid soðre bletsunge, ond on merigenlicere tide mynster gesohte. Weard þa se munuc micclum afyrht, ond adlig on aernemerigen hine geeadmette to ðaes halgan cneowum, biddende þaet he his adl eallunge afligde ond his fyrwitnysse faederlice miltsode. Se halga ða sona andwyrde: "Ic ðinum gedwylde dearnunge miltsige, gif ðu ða gesihðe mid swigan bediglast oðþaet min sawul heonon sidige of andwerdum life geladod to heofonan." Cuðberhtus ða mid gebede his sceaweres seocnysse gehaelde ond his fyrwites ganges gylt forgeaf.

(This said holy man was accustomed to go at night to the beach and stand in the salt sea up to his neck chanting his prayer. One summer's night another monk listened for him to pass by and, stalking him stealthily, followed his footsteps, until both came to the beach. Then did Cuthbert, as he was accustomed, chant his prayer standing in the sea up to his neck, and afterwards he bent his knees upon the sand and stretched out his palms to the heavens. And lo, two seals came up from the bottom of the sea, and with their fur they dried his feet, and with their breaths warmed his body, and then with a sign asked his blessing as they lay at his feet on the brown sand. Then Cuthbert sent the sea-beasts back into the sea with a true blessing, and in the morning returned to the monastery. The monk was then afraid, and being ill early in the morning, humbled himself upon his knees before the saint, praying him to drive away his illness and show a fatherly compassion upon his curiosity. The saint thereupon answered him, saying, "I will privately forgive your error if you will keep the things you have seen a secret until my soul, being summoned to heaven, shall depart hence out of this present life." Cuthbert then by prayer healed the sickness of his spy, and forgave him his blameworthy curiosity.) [3]

We shall see in a moment what the tumbling style looks like in a pamphleteer. It does not appear in full bloom until the Elizabethan period, and when it does, three sources are discernible in it: informal conversation, as of the tavern or market place, alliterative-accentual poetry (i.e., the "tumbling verse" of numerous poets from *Piers Plowman* to Shakespeare, the best of it well laced with humor), and the popular sermon. But the style that we can identify so distinctly in the pamphlets of the Marprelate controversy and in almost every piece of prose written by Thomas Nashe and Gabriel Harvey has unmistakable precedent in the Lollard tracts contemporaneous with *Piers Plowman*; and its evolution can be traced through a long line of pamphlets, sermons, and poems of popular flavor extending through the fifteenth and sixteenth centuries. The history of the pamphlet literature has been ably handled by Professor G. P. Krapp, whose chapters on it deserve careful reading.

"Wyclif," says Mr. Krapp, "took truth out of the hands of authoritative dogmatists, and put it into the hands of all those who were earnestly seeking for truth"; "he removed it from the regions of the fixed and the absolute, and placed it on the battlefield of popular debate and opinion." "Debate," he continues, "which had hitherto been carried on only in the high altitudes of technical and disciplined scholarship, was now to descend to the level of popular speech and of the popular mind, undrilled and untaught in the subtleties of logic, but often making up for these deficiencies by earnestness of purpose, by breadth of human interest, and by a vivacity of feeling which somehow seems to evaporate at the higher levels." [4]

Now one thing that the tumbling style never fails to imply is the speaking voice; and it is very significant that as criticism entered the popular arena, the defender of new, anti-authoritarian causes often appeared as a dramatized, fictitious character, belonging always, of course, to the humbler ranks of society. That is what we see in the person of Langland's Plowman; and Piers set the example for the hero of a group of tracts of the first decade of the fifteenth century and later for him of the Marprelate quarrel. The earlier of these two battlers was Jack Upland. The Jack Upland tracts are debates between Jack and another imaginary character, Friar Daw Topias. Professor Krapp describes the medium of their dispute as "a rhythmical kind of alliterating prose," "printed as verse by the editor, but really the kind of tumbling prose which so often resulted from the popular and loose treatment of the older alliterative long line," a prose salted with homespun words and phrases ("as lewd as a leek," "I know not an A from the wind-mill, nor a B from a bull-foot") [5] — altogether a prose of the utmost liveliness and good nature.

The example of Piers and Jack can be seen in the imaginary and nameless interlocutor with whom Sir Thomas More provides himself in his famous *Dialogue* against "the pestilent sect of Luther and Tyndale," published in 1529.[6] This person is a rough-and-ready partisan of reform, and it argues a curious lapse from the usual sagacity of the great humanist that he should have given his opponent the well-loved character by now associated with homespun talk, for in the *Dialogue* the speaker named Thomas More is meant to prevail. How much better strategy he employed in *Utopia*, where the arguments of the speaker named Thomas More are clearly meant to be pulverized by the explorer Raphael Hythloday.

The *Dialogue* certainly did nothing to deter the Reformers of the next generation from once again committing their cause to a new fictitious spokesman of the old stamp, Martin Marprelate. Who invented the character is not known, but we can see in several tracts connected with the name the most opulent display of the tumbling manner in prose to date and writers who are very conscious stylists. The spirit of the controversy is that of the old-fashioned flyting, wherein both sides are more intent upon putting on a show and making the other side look foolish than in the serious merits of the points at issue, a spirit that persists into the pamphlet wars of the next century (readers of Milton's tracts are aware that these are no exception); though nowhere, as it happens, from the Marprelate side do we get quite such wild antics as in Lyly's *Pappe with a Hatchet* or in any of the pamphlets of Nashe. These highly educated writers were evidently determined to outdo the homespun fellows in their own vein. Nashe warmed to the style as he developed, so that his later pieces "tumble" with more commotion than the early ones, wherein he has not yet altogether thrown off the general contemporary habit of euphuizing. It may be, as Professor Krapp argues, that Martin's performance in the controversy was in some sense "superior" to that of Lyly, Nashe, or Richard Harvey;[7] but if we would see the full resources of the tumbler's art, Nashe is the man for our money. His massed stresses are heftier and he is more fluent in word-coining, wider-ranging in his affectation of a backslapping familiarity with learned lore, and bolder in his coarse, slangy diction. The American journalist of today can open Nashe's pages at random and recognize his own style as if in a mirror: its cheerful energy and the inexhaustible novelty of its facetious phrasing, imagery, and allusions. Needless to say, a little of it goes a long way for any but the reader with a skin an inch thick. Here, for a taste of Nashe at his best, is the conclusion of his version of the touching tale of Hero and Leander:

Downe shee ranne in her loose night-gowne, and her haire about her eares (euen as Semiramis ranne out with her lie-pot in her hand,

and her blacke dangling tresses about her shoulders with her iuory combe ensnarled in them, when she heard that Babilon was taken), and thought to haue kist his dead corse aliue againe, but as on his blew iellied sturgeon lips she was about to clappe one of those warme plaisters, boystrous woolpacks of ridged tides came rowling in, and raught him from her, (with a minde belike to carrie him backe to Abidos.) At that she became a franticke Bacchanal outright, & made no more bones but spra[n]g after him, and so resignd vp her Priesthood, and left worke for Musæus and Kit Marlowe. The gods, and goddesses all on a rowe, bread and crow, from Ops to Pomona, the first applewife, were so dumpt with this miserable wracke, that they beganne to abhorre al moysture for the seas sake: and Iupiter could not endure Ganimed, his cup-bearer, to come in his presence, both for the dislike he bore to Neptunes baneful licour, as also that hee was so like to Leander. The sunne was so in his mumps vppon it, that it was almost noone before hee could goe to cart that day, and then with so ill a will hee went, that hee had thought to haue topled his burning carre or Hurrie currie into the sea (as Phaeton did) to scorch it and dry it vppe, and at night, when hee was begrimed with dust and sweate of his iourney, he would not descend as he was woont, to wash him in the Ocean, but vnder a tree layde him downe to rest in his cloathes all night, and so did the scouling Moone vnder another fast by him, which of that [i.e., consequently] are behighted the trees of the Sunne and Moone, and are the same that Syr Iohn Mandeuile tels vs hee spoke with, and that spoke to Alexander.[8]

The pounding of crowded stressed and half-stressed syllables stands out in virtually every news item on the sports pages of our newspapers. The accentuation of the prose is often what that of the old native poetry would be if its rules had allowed, amongst other types of half-line, types with the non-fully-stressed syllables reduced to one only or to none. And it will be recalled that even the classical rules admitted a good many extra syllables of this kind and that one meets expanded half-lines (i.e., half-lines containing three full stresses) in several of the Anglo-Saxon poems. The following extract from a sports article of twenty years ago, which I have laid out to look like verse, will be recognized as quite typical in its rhythm, as also in the facetious tone of voice with which it makes a learned allusion.

PROSE STYLES

For the second time   during this young season

Old Man   Jupiter Pluvius

washed out   the entire major league

baseball day   schedule Thursday.

With twenty-one   playing days

Of the season gone by   the sixteen

big league teams   already have been plagued

with forty-five   postponements

twenty-four   in the National league

and twenty-one   in the American [league].

But a distinctly tumbling style has also been cultivated by more than one writer of belletristic pretensions in our century, among others the late Bernard DeVoto, in whom one seems to sense the inspiration of the old *American Mercury.* In the following passage from DeVoto's novel *We Accept with Pleasure*, the allusions and the subdued humor offer a fine contrast to the journalist's effort just quoted, and half a dozen times we hear an almost perfectly classical alliterative-accentual half-line. Is not this the way — except for the sophisticated element in the thought — in which a pre-Conquest scop would compose in modern English?

Chicago stank. Limp asphalt, offal, swamps — blend of exhaust fumes, human sweat, the flowing blood of steers. The smell of a metropolis, unclean, inescapable, heroic. The editor's windows opened on Michigan Avenue, on blue heat, on the ant heap of Grant Park, the tracks, the made land beyond them, and at last the lake. There was, at last, the lake. Far out the smoke from an ore boat was a ruled line miles long, motionless. Nearer a tri-motor plane angled into sight and, climbing, headed eastward. White smoke edged with blue fell away from it in puffs. Ore boat and plane would make their gifts of stench. Air would be fouler still on the street, where noise passed beyond the ear's octave and was a throbbing felt centrally in the blood. Stench, noise, and the heat of prairies untouched by wind. . . .

He shook her hand and, hastily, went out . . . Prairie heat was a wall he forced himself against. He walked through jagged clamor. Chicago screamed, whore of cities.

Traffic stopped in geometric lines at the spot of red in a lamp. Loring walked dryshod the divided sea. Tires hummed, endlessly rocking. A monoplane pink with sunset, roared in a nose dive, flipped over, straightened out, belched yellow gases and made off. Traffic heaved forward and the tires whirred.[9]

Since the more stress-crowded rhythmic units that I have seen as distinctive — indeed, as the main feature — of tumbling discourse are among the handiest of means by which one may impart urgency to any expression of suitable length, they naturally turn up here and there in various kinds of spoken and written prose other than the one of which they supply the essential earmark. We identify the thing properly to be called the tumbling type of prose when these units (along with those other elements of style that I have associated with them) make themselves felt as expressing the speaker's sustained and prevailing point of view.

A people may pride itself upon both its consciously cultivated manners and what it believes to be the natural, uncultivated core of its character. The tumbling style is the instinctive expression of the speaker who, whether throughout a discourse of some length or only for a passing remark, seems to proclaim himself the forthright English yeoman, the hearty repudiator of all frills and graces, all convention, all illusion ("He'll win hands down — and I don't mean maybe"; "The big boss — is a stuffed shirt"; "Three two-baggers — in one inning"; " 'Pooh! pooh!' cries the squire — 'all stuff and non-sense' "; "his horse hipped — with an old mossy saddle — . . . past cure of the fives — stark spoiled with the staggers — . . . near-legged before — with a half-checked bit . . .''; "Don't tell me — that men aren't liars"). Other tongues besides English have their own ways of expressing a similar point of view, especially those of the Germanic family; but we also hear the emphasis of crowded stresses in French in a plain-spoken phrase here and there (witness Rabelais's Frère Jan: "Mille diables," "ho Diable," "Feste Dieu," "Mgna, gna, gna, dist frere Jan. Fy qu'il est laid, le pleurant de merde. Mousse, ho, de par tous les Diables, garde l'escantoula"); [10] and salty objurgations are no monopoly of any language. But can any language match the rich monosyllabic resources of English to box a fellow's ears with? May not one even fancy a connection between the percussive effects that English can render and the ancient English taste for fisticuffs and the singlestick, whether for sport or serious combat?

The pieces I have discussed provide food for profound meditation on the morality of that element of the English genius that their style expresses. Do the sterling virtues of our native culture include humility? I seem to remember that King Hrothgar in *Beowulf* says of his predecessor on the throne, "se waes betera ðonne ic" — "he was a better man than I" — and I daresay a good many like illustrations could be cited; but neither *Beowulf* nor any of the surviving versions of other Anglo-Saxon poems antedates the influence of Christianity, and in much of this poetry, as in most of the tumbling verse and prose of later times, whatever the words say, the manner is by no means that of humility or restraint but that of an unflagging, often aggressive, self-assurance. Self-assurance is a virtue, too, no doubt, of a sort, and even the blatant kind implied by our style where it is most unlike other styles appeals powerfully to us when we are in a mood to breathe deep, flex our muscles, and tell the world to go to hell; but the mood is too highflying to last long, and the style, if forced, can be painfully tiresome. Tumbling prose, even the comic kind, is best taken in short measures. One soon wearies of the thumping accents, the blunt words, the pumped-up periphrases, the swagger, the impudence. I began by noticing that Anglo-Saxon verses can be undulating and graceful, but graceful ones do not make the characteristic music of Anglo-Saxon poetry, and still less that of modern tumbling prose.

If we English-speaking peoples had not learned most of our modern styles in prose and verse from classical and romance sources, the imagination shrivels to think that the "Finnsburg Fragment," excellent of its kind though it be, might fairly represent the range of our capacity for articulate thought and sentiment. In the samples of tumbling discourse I have cited we have a negative but conveniently concrete reminder of the virtues of our mongrel heritage. We may rejoice, surely, in the Anglo-Saxon part of it, and still recognize how wanting in scope would be a thoroughbred modern Anglo-Saxon literature.

I shall return, in closing, to the question with which I began, namely, whether the tumbling style can properly be regarded as of parallel order with the other styles I have distinguished. Does it differ in some functional way from other narrative styles?

I can only repeat that I have the impression of a dynamism in prose conspicuously marked with the features I have been describing that is indeed unique in nonmetrical discourse: the dynamism of the scop as opposed to the more deliberate motives of narrative writers whose style approximates that of the debater or that of the teacher or preacher or that of the prophet. Whether or not in verse, tumbling discourse is poetry: it imposes (or seeks to impose) its effects, like any of the genres that the word "poetry" calls first to mind, by inducing in the addressee from the very start a state of heightened susceptibility to feeling. A "tumbling" tale does not, like a narrative by Thucydides or George Eliot, invite attention to its reasonableness as it progresses; it is not so consciously faithful to fact or to the exigencies of practical didacticism as a shipmaster's log or a chronicle; nor is its challenge that of a cool, enigmatic narrative by a George Meredith or a Wyndham Lewis.

The writer leaps into his performance like an acrobat or a clown (as the word "tumbling" suggests): witness the "Hwæt!" with which at least two of the Anglo-Saxon poems begin (*Beowulf* and the so-called "Dream of the Rood"), the inverted word order at the beginning of the paragraph I have quoted from Nashe ("Downe shee ranne in her loose night-gowne"), and the abrupt, shock opening of the paragraph from Bernard DeVoto's novel ("Chicago stank"). Once launched, the pace is all bounce and tumult, and nothing counts so much as the sustaining of it at a breakneck pace from moment to moment. Here is Gulliver explaining the economics of England to the Houyhnhnm his master:

Hence it follows of necessity, that vast numbers of our people are compelled to seek their livelihood by begging, robbing, stealing, cheating, pimping, forswearing, flattering, suborning, forging, gaming, lying, fawning, hectoring, voting, scribbling, star-gazing, poisoning, whoring, canting, libelling, freethinking, and the like occupations . . .[11]

Here is a Japanese medical experimenter in Smollett's *The Adventures of an Atom*:

He therefore tried the method of gentle friction: for which purpose he used almost the very same substances which were many centuries after applied by Gargantua to his own posteriors: such as a nightcap, a pillow-bier, a slipper, a poke, a panier, a beaver, a hen, a cock, a chicken, a calf-skin, a hare-skin, a pigeon, a cormorant, a lawyer's bag, a lamprey, a coif, a lure . . . [etc.][12]

The sputter of rapid-fire conversation is a common tumbling expedient, something conspicuous on nearly every page of *Tristram Shandy*:

—— Bonjour! —— good morrow! —— so you have got your cloak on betimes! —— but 'tis a cold morning, and you judge the matter rightly —— 'tis better to be well mounted, than go o' foot —— and obstructions in the glands are dangerous —— And how goes it with thy concubine —— thy wife, —— and thy little ones o' both sides? and when did you hear from the old gentleman and lady —— your sister, aunt, uncle, and cousins —— I hope they have got better of their colds, coughs, claps, tooth-aches, fevers, stranguries, sciaticas, swellings, and sore eyes.[13]

Of Sterne, Paul Stapfer remarked that whereas "Il y a du dieu dans Rabelais, — du diable aussi: dans Sterne il y a du singe."[14] I wonder if the tumbling vein does not imply something of the simian in many another writer besides Sterne, not excepting even Rabelais.

Each of the other styles I have defined is addressed either mainly to the intellect or, if and insofar as to the emotions, always by way of the intellect; but tumbling prose, like an old-fashioned lyric or ballad, batters at the seat of feeling directly from the start; and its language, even if witty or facetiously erudite, is easy to the point of transparence. If it run to jargon or gibberish, the intended challenge of this lies not to our powers of comprehension but directly to the funny bone. It is a shock-assault, a blitz. Heads up! it says, stand clear! In Br'er Rabbit's language: "Gimme room! Tu'n me loose! I'm ole man Spewter-Splutter wid long claws, en scales on my back! I'm snaggle-toofed en double-j'inted! Gimme room!"[15]

If any kind of persuasion be intended, this must be oblique. Feeling can come straight, thought only aslant. We can enjoy taking in the writer's ideas, whatever they be, so long as his manner makes plain our freedom to discount him for a clown or a crank; but he loses us any time he expects us to take his bluster at par. The literary duel of Nashe and Gabriel Harvey in the 1590's was a good show of its kind, but Nashe, who proves himself intelligent enough to have known better, must be judged more the angry child than the competent fencer when he says, "thou beest a goosecap and hast no judgment" or "it cannot be but thou liest, learned Gabriel" (in *Strange News*, 1592). The fun of men like H. L. Mencken or George Jean Nathan or Bernard DeVoto is that we can nearly always chuckle over their philippics and not care a pin who or what they are for or against.

Like it or not, the roots of this style lie deep in the genius of the English language and all that it stands for. First appearing in prose as a conscious imitation, indeed a relaxed variant, of the style of our primitive poetry, its features at all times recall its origin to any student of that poetry; yet it is to be doubted that today more than one writer of it in a dozen, if that many, has any knowledge of its earlier history or writes it with any conscious sense of emulating any model of prose (or verse) older than the work of his living contemporaries. I can find no evidence of its use in print during the long interval between the later Renaissance pamphleteers and the twentieth century, except such short, incidental passages as I have quoted from Swift, Smollett, and Sterne; and I seem to see it reborn within living memory as a current, standard style for the sports page as if by spontaneous generation. Its emergence here seems to be not much older than the First World War, for prior to that time our sports articles were much more redolent of the genteel prose of the nineteenth century, rich in polysyllabic diction, euphemism, and other marks of decorum that look stilted today, than prophetic of the prose of Mencken or Bernard DeVoto. Needless to say, the subject could do with further investigation.

THE PROPHETIC STYLE

Biblical Prophecy · Stoic Philosophy · The Essay

And it came to pass, when Jesus had ended these sayings, the
people were astonished at his doctrine:
For he taught them as one having authority, and not as the scribes.
— Matthew vii.28–29

AN ASSORTMENT of loosely related aphorisms is the essential
substance of a work of prophecy. The force of the whole is the
self-contained force of these separate units, or mainly so.

The force of the single aphorism is the immediate plausibility of
it. We take it or leave it as it stands. The idea expressed, apart from
the form, is likely to be most impressive if it is original. Commonplaces are impressive too, but it needs no prophet to retail them. A
cento of commonplaces suggests a compiler rather than a prophet.
Prophets take us by surprise by laying down paradoxes as laws, both
descriptive and prescriptive. "Ye have heard that it hath been said,
An eye for an eye, and a tooth for a tooth: But I say unto you, That
ye resist not evil: but whosoever shall smite thee on thy right cheek,
turn to him the other also."

But commonplaces have their use in prophecy too, for their already established authority lends extra weight to accompanying paradoxes by association.

Having stated an aphorism, the prophet may go on, as in the
passage just quoted, to state an application of it; but when he does,
it is typically for the purpose of illustration rather than of logical

proof. The truth or virtue of it we are to accept without proof; if we refuse, that ends the matter. There can be no dispute, as with the conclusions of a reasoner, which, standing always in logical relations with premises, allow, nay, invite, analysis and criticism. One may deny a prophet's aphorisms and offer reasons for doing so, but there is no controverting an opponent who, as his style announces, has repudiated reason in advance and stands upon his intuitions alone. The choice for the addressee boils down to whether he will say "amen" or throw bricks.

Where we are concerned with reasoning, we recognize that the ultimate grounds of any position may lie anywhere within the whole continuum of experience; and it is the way of good reasoners to allow for this fact. We expect any argument, especially one of the deliberative sort, to have a certain fulness and to be expressed in an unhurried style. It cannot, of course, defend all of its possible implications, but fulness can make it seem the result of wide consideration, and to that extent weighty and wise.

But in prophecy it is terseness that carries conviction, for terseness implies that the thing said *needs* no defense. It is the best of ways in which the prophet may proclaim his freedom and invite disciples to join him on heights where the vision is unimpeded by the smoke and stir of debate.

Brief expressions have to be categorical, and paradoxes are striking and stimulating precisely because they contain no room for reservations or apologies. Prophets love to emphasize the brevity of their pronouncements by making each stand somewhat apart in sense from its context, for even a short and grammatically independent proposition may lose some of the virtue of its brevity if it bear some close and apparent relation in sense to neighboring ones. Here, says Brevity, is the truth: let the wise receive it and be grateful; it is not for fools. "He that refuseth instruction despiseth his own soul: but he that heareth reproof getteth understanding" (Proverbs xv.32).

Brevity and disjointedness are therefore no accident of the prophetic style, but primary features of it. Prophecy is neither superior to argument nor inferior: it is a different order of discourse. It is the substance of what we call the Prophetic Books of the Bible, of the primary documents of Stoic philosophy, and of what, beginning with Montaigne, has been known throughout modern times as the "essay." No better term than essay could be applied to such texts (or sections thereof) as the *Encheiridion* of Epictetus or the *Epistolae* and so-called *Dialogi* of Seneca; and there is much of both the spirit and style of prophecy in certain poems that have been called "essays," notably those of Pope.

Though Stoicism, as a philosophy known by that name, originated among the Greeks, it is, I believe, generally understood to be less characteristic of Greek thought in general than of Roman; but the resemblance between the style of Stoic prose, both Greek and Roman, and that of biblical prophecy can probably be seen as a fair measure of the debt that the pioneer Greek Stoics owed to oriental predecessors. The Greek genius, it has been said, is characterized above all things "by a love for and faith in reason," by "the faculty of seeing both sides of a question." [1] The Stoic thinkers, on the other hand, while asserting, in the usual Greek way, their faith in reason, in fact sought the truth, not by way of what we ordinarily think of as a rational approach, but in flashes of inner illumination. Their style in prose composition, moreover, so far from resembling the lucid, coherent, and fully articulate prose of a Plato or an Aristotle, is concentrated, elliptical, and metaphorical.

That it should run to metaphor is both un-Greek in general and notably at variance with principles that the Stoics themselves professed, for metaphor is a dramatic and exciting mode of expression, and the Stoics, instead of taking the moderate Greek view that emotion is something to be held under control, pretended to allow no place for it whatever in the good life. Their radicalism on this point was quite un-Greek in spirit, and their style strangely inconsistent with their own ethical doctrine.

The several inconsistencies, including this one, that critics have pointed out in Stoic philosophy are indeed striking, yet it is questionable whether any of the other ancient systems has had a more important or enduring influence. It is understood to have been the most generally received philosophy among educated Romans from the second century B.C. forward; it is deeply involved in Christian thought; and the men of the Middle Ages and the Renaissance never ceased to draw fresh inspiration from pagan Stoic authors. The chief preserver of its most vital ideas for the modern world has undoubtedly been the Christian church. Since no better tag than "Stoic" could be used to designate the philosophical point of view implied by the style presently under consideration, it would be interesting to linger on the many affinities between Stoicism and Christianity that have been recognized. Suffice it to notice that E. Vernon Arnold has treated the subject with some fulness in his work on Roman Stoicism, emphasizing how thoroughly St. Paul was "steeped in Stoic ways of thinking" and how much in the nature of revolutionary Stoic paradoxes are such cornerstones of Christian doctrine as the ideas of life as death, death as life, and the master as servant.[2]

Stoic prose was anticipated in some of its features by that of the more informal speeches in the Platonic dialogues. It is not, however, quite the same thing. Socrates clearly believes that truth once grasped is generally reducible to orderly expression. But the truths that count most in the eyes of the Stoics are "veiled," as Mr. Croll says, "from common observation" beneath layers of "illusory appearances" and are revealed only in flashes and only to the rarest minds.[3] The business of the Stoic seer is to catch what he can of the ever new but fleeting visions presented to him, a chosen vessel, as in a kaleidoscope, by a cosmos in a constant state of motion.

It was a notable event when the Stoics asserted the source of all things to be a divine power in a state of eternal activity. Here was a metaphysics for the whole race of malcontents, plain dealers, Calvinists, and the like: for every man who goes about with a thorn in his foot or a flea in his ear. Given a cosmos in constant motion, the thing that matters most is what comes next. Philosophy becomes a kind of footrace, and philosophers fiercely jealous of their prowess and contemptuous of all pedestrian or popular modes of discourse. The truth must be seized before it has had time to move or change, therefore on the instant; and if so, the expression must be impromptu and dramatic. The expression will tend to render the activity of conception rather than the idea conceived.[4]

[73]

The style of typical Stoic writers is best explained by the principle just described, for it only in part illustrates the stated principles of the school. Here is a set of rules attributed by Diogenes Laertius to Diogenes the Babylonian:

There are five excellences of speech — pure Greek, lucidity, conciseness, appropriateness, distinction. By good Greek is meant language faultless in point of grammar and free from careless vulgarity. Lucidity is a style which presents the thought in a way easily understood; conciseness a style that employs no more words than are necessary for setting forth the subject in hand; appropriateness lies in a style akin to the subject; distinction in the avoidance of colloquialism.[5]

It has been remarked (by G. L. Hendrickson and also by M. W. Croll) that the kind of appropriateness here called for is not, as with Aristotle and Cicero, appropriateness to the addressee and the occasion, but only to the subject.[6] But the subject in typical Stoic discourse, as we have seen, is rather the activity of the writer's mind than anything external to him; so it follows that an appropriate style must necessarily be highly individual. The rule of conciseness, of course, applies as stated. That of lucidity could not be taken as binding upon a writer whose first object is to be faithful to moments of vision caught on the wing, to render which he may need to resort to difficult images, ellipses, and the like. The rules relating to purity of language and the avoidance of colloquialism seem hardly relevant at all, though we can understand why in recommending a new style a theorist might go out of his way to profess these scruples. The unimportance attached to them by the Stoics is evident from Zeno's remark "that the very exact expressions used by those who avoided solecisms were like the coins struck by Alexander: they were beautiful in appearance and well rounded like the coins, but none the better on that account. Words of the opposite kind he would compare to the Attic tetradrachms [sic], which though struck carelessly and inartistically, nevertheless outweighed the ornate phrases";[7] and we are told that Chrysippus, in his work *On the Ancient Natural Philosophers*, treated the myth of Hera and Zeus in "language . . . more appropriate to street-walkers than to deities."[8] Cicero said of the Roman Stoic Quintus Aelius Tubero that, as in his personal life, so in his oratory, he was "severe, uncouth, and rough," and he finds the Stoics in general given to excessive terseness and to a dryness and obscurity eloquent of their attitude of cool indifference toward the common people.[9]

The following paragraph from the *Discourses* of Epictetus begins with a string of questions, with an occasional word in answer from an imagined interlocutor, but when a full-length answer is given, the questioner supplies it in his own person. It is all "I" and "you," but mostly "I." It is aphoristic and imperative. Objects of reference range from Hercules the master of lions to indigestion. The tone of voice is that of a "fight-talk," as if the battle of philosophy hung on a desperate chance. The writer is in a hurry, and though he can be terse, he can also waste words (one adjective would hit as hard as the four used in the penultimate sentence). And does he not take rather special delight in warning us that a man may die suffering such an unmentionable affliction as a "dysentery"?

Where the room for, *How will it be? What will be the event?* And *Will this happen, or that?* Is not the event uncontrollable by will? "Yes." And does not the essence of good and evil consist in what is within the control of will? It is in your power, then, to treat every event conformably to Nature? Can any one restrain you? "No one." Then do not say to me any more, *How will it be?* For, however it be, you will set it right, and the event to you will be auspicious.

Pray what would Hercules have been, if he had said, "What can be done to prevent a great lion, or a large boar, or savage men, from coming in my way?" Why, what is that to you? If a large boar should come in your way, you will fight the greater combat; if wicked men, you will deliver the world from wicked men. "But then if I should die by this means?" You will die as a good man, in the performance of a gallant action. For since, at all events, one must die, one must necessarily be found doing something, either tilling, or digging, or trading, or serving a consulship, or sick with indigestion or dysentery. At what employment, then, would you have death find you? For my part, I would have it to be some humane, beneficent, public-spirited, noble action. But if I cannot be found doing any such great things, yet, at least, I would be doing what I am incapable of being restrained from, what is given me to do, — correcting myself, improving that faculty which makes use of the phenomena of existence to procure tranquillity, and render to the several relations of life their due; and if I am so fortunate, advancing still further to the security of judging right.[10]

Lucius Annaeus Seneca, the most fluent and exciting of the Roman spokesmen of Stoicism, was undoubtedly the chief source of the Stoic influence in medieval and Renaissance times. John W. Basore, editor and translator of the Loeb edition of the *Epistolae Morales*, speaks of these as "quasi-dialogues," on the ground that they are "developed with vague consciousness of an argumentative second person." [11]

Seneca's writings were read and admired, translated and quoted, on every hand from his own time to the age of the Enlightenment, in spite of critics who found fault with his style.[12] Quintilian thought his phraseology in bad taste, and deplored his "petty attempts at sententiousness." [13] To the Emperor Caligula his speeches were "sand without lime"; [14] and every student of the age of Dryden and Pope has probably encountered the complaint of the third Earl of Shaftesbury (1711) that the Senecan "Canterbury or amble" had been a model of style so much emulated during the preceding hundred years that "we have scarce the idea of any other." [15] For a brief sample, here is a paragraph from Seneca's letter to his brother Novatus on anger, a quasi-dialogue, of which the Latin is almost as dense and disjointed as a telegram:

"At enim ira habet aliquam voluptatem et dulce est dolorem reddere." Minime: non enim ut in beneficiis honestum est merita meritis repensare, ita iniurias iniuriis. Illic vinci turpe est, his vincere. Inhumanum verbum est et quidem pro iusto receptum ultio, et talio non multum differt nisi ordine; qui dolorem regerit tantum excusatius peccat. M. Catonem ignorans in balineo quidam percussit imprudens; quis enim illi sciens faceret iniuriam? Postea satis facienti Cato: "Non memini," inquit, "me percussum." Melius putavit non agnoscere quam vindicare. "Nihil," inquis, "illi post tantam petulantiam mali factum est?" Immo multum boni; coepit Catonem nosse. Magni animi est iniurias despicere; ultionis contumeliosissimum genus est non esse visum dignum, ex quo peteretur ultio. Multi leves iniurias altius sibi demisere, dum vindicant. Ille magnus et nobilis, qui more magnae ferae latratus minutorum canum securus exaudit.

("But then there is something pleasurable in anger, and it is sweet

[76]

to give back pain for pain?" By no means; for it is not honorable to return injuries for injuries as it is, in the way of kindness, to return favors for favors. In the latter case it is shameful to be outdone, in the former not to be. "Revenge" is an inhuman word, and yet commonly received as legitimate, and "retaliation in kind" differs little from it except in order; whoso retaliates in kind merely sins with more claim to be pardoned for so doing. A certain fellow once struck Marcus Cato in the bath, not knowing who he was; for who would knowingly have injured that great man? Then, as he was apologizing, Cato said: "I do not remember having been struck." He thought it better to ignore than resent the incident. "Then the fellow got no punishment," you may say, "for such rude behavior?" No: instead he was richly rewarded; he began to know Cato. It is the part of the great soul to be superior to injuries. The most telling penalty to suffer is not to seem to be worthy of another's vengeance. Many have taken slight injuries too seriously by avenging them. He is great and noble who, like a great wild beast, listens unperturbed to the barking of small dogs.) [16]

It will be seen that the point of view comes out here much better in the Latin than in the translation; but in Bacon's *Essays*, the English classic in this vein, the language leaves nothing to be desired. The following passage could hardly be bettered as a textbook specimen of the style, though it could hardly have been written by any but a seasoned Latinist:

What is Truth; said jesting Pilate; And would not stay for an Answer. Certainly there be, that delight in Giddiness; And count it a Bondage, to fix a Beleefe; Affecting Free-Will in Thinking, as well as in Acting. And though the Sects of Philosophers of that Kinde be gone, yet there remaine certaine discoursing Wits, which are of the same veines, though there be not so much Bloud in them, as was in those of the Ancients. But it is not onely the Difficultie, and Labour, which Men take in finding out of Truth; Nor againe, that when it is found, it imposeth vpon mens Thoughts; that doth bring Lies in fauour: But a naturall, though corrupt Loue, of the Lie it selfe. One of the later Schoole of the Grecians, examineth the matter, and is at a stand, to thinke what should be in it, that men should loue Lies; Where neither they make for Pleasure, as with Poets; Nor for Aduantage, as with the Merchant; but for the Lies sake. But I cannot tell: This same Truth, is a Naked, and Open day light, that doth not shew, the Masques, and Mummeries, and Triumphs of the world, halfe so Stately, and daintily, as Candlelights. Truth may perhaps come to the price of a Pearle, that sheweth best by day: But it will not rise, to the price of a Diamond, or Carbuncle, that sheweth best in varied lights. A mixture of a Lie doth euer adde Pleasure. Doth any man doubt, that if there were taken out of Mens Mindes, Vaine Opinions, Flattering Hopes, False Valuations, Imaginations as one would, and the like; but it would leaue the Mindes, of a Number of Men, poore shrunken Things; full of Melancholy, and Indisposition, and vnpleasing to themselues? One of the Fathers, in great Seuerity, called Poesie, Vinum Daemonum; because it filleth the Imagination, and yet it is but with the shadow of a Lie. But it is not the Lie, that passeth through the Minde, but the Lie that sinketh in, and setleth in it, that doth the hurt, such as we spake of before.[17]

It is one of Croll's many illuminating insights that while the original impulse of the Stoic seer is to be terse (or *coupé*), in the way of Bacon, his type is also recognizable in the copious, loose (or *décousu*) prose of men like Montaigne or Sir Thomas Browne. Browne's sentences seem to acknowledge more of premeditation than those of Bacon, but he is quite as full of surprises and delights to challenge the reader — not to embarrass but to flatter him — with the most recondite of learned words and allusions. The well-known conclusion of *The Garden of Cyrus* (1658) is a fair specimen of a mainly *décousu* style:

But the quincunx of heaven runs low, and 'tis time to close the five ports of knowledge. We are unwilling to spin out our awaking thoughts into the phantasms of sleep, which often continueth precogitations; making cables of cobwebs, and wildernesses of handsome groves. Beside Hippocrates hath spoke so little, and the oneirocritical masters have left such frigid interpretations from plants, that there is little encouragement to dream of Paradise itself. Nor will the sweetest delight of gardens afford much comfort in sleep; wherein the dulness of that sense shakes hands with delectable odours; and though in the bed of Cleopatra, can hardly with any delight raise up the ghost of a rose.

Night, which Pagan theology could make the daughter of Chaos, affords no advantage to the description of order; although no lower than that mass can we derive its genealogy. All things began in order, so shall they end, and so shall they begin again; according to the ordainer of order and mystical mathematicks of the city of heaven. Though Somnus in Homer be sent to rouse up Agamemnon, I find no such effects in these drowsy approaches of sleep. To keep our eyes open longer, were but to act our Antipodes. The huntsmen are up in America, and they are already past their first sleep in Persia. But who can be drowsy at that hour which first freed us from ever-lasting sleep? or have slumbering thoughts at that time, when sleep itself must end, and as some conjecture all shall awake again?[18]

The first great wave of English essay writing, that of the seventeenth century, inclined prevailingly to this loose, meandering style; but though any use of the word "essay" to designate a prose work is an ostensible protestation of modesty on the writer's part, his typical message is an implied declaration of independence — of irresponsibility, in the old-fashioned sense. In any essay properly so-called the writer goes his own way, more boldly in the terse kind, sometimes inclining to truculence, and commonly with good nature and often a measure of humor in the copious, loose variety.

Bacon's remark that there is not so much blood in the modern "discoursing wits" as there was in the ancients suggests the broad reflection that any ancient thinker was in a position to lay down the law more confidently about large philosophical issues than any has been in the modern age, when quantitative science and the wide dissemination of the printed word have required him to come to terms with an ever more forbidding system of established fact and therefore with an ever more sharply critical court of public opinion. In the new age there were to be fewer daredevils than formerly who, like Bacon, were ready to venture upon the wholesale invention of serious aphorisms on any and all subjects. The race of Montaigne, Burton, and Browne, later revived in Charles Lamb and his following, was cannier. The primary motive in these writers is still oracular and often revolutionary, but the style is discreet, cagey, devious, often jocular. They hurl no old-fashioned challenge at us, to make us think that our fate depends on our assent to their doctrine.

But on fingering over several collections of nineteenth- and twentieth-century essays, I have been somewhat surprised to find no very lengthy passages in the meandering manner so characteristic of the seventeenth-century men. Here and there I find two or three lengthy, loose sentences together in a writer like Robert Louis Stevenson or

Logan Pearsall Smith, but that is all. Can it be that the leisurely, sprawling manner became an anachronism with the advent of the age of steam? Even with Lamb, the clock never quite stopped: in most of his writing the movement is nervous and quick. Exceptions apart, the nineteenth-century essayists run more to energy than to measured contemplation; their taste is more for curt periods of a more or less playful tone than for either the sprawling sentence or the curt sentence that is wholly serious. Emerson is an exception of course: he can be both curt and sober, like Bacon or Tacitus; more so, I believe, than any other man of his century one could name.

In the following passage from Robert Louis Stevenson — the second sentence — we can see what the *décousu* style looks like in a writer of the fairly recent past. The pressure here is gentle: the writer connects the several main members of the sentence and the two parts of the last main member by loose connectives ("but," "and," "and," "and"). The trailing effect of the two concluding participial phrases is also interesting:

When the old man waggles his head and says, "Ah, so I thought when I was your age," he has proved the youth's case. Doubtless, whether from growth of experience or decline of animal heat, he thinks so no longer; but he thought so while he was young; and all men have thought so while they were young, since there was dew in the morning or hawthorn in May; and here is another young man adding his vote to those of previous generations and riveting another link to the chain of testimony.[19]

Or listen to Logan Pearsall Smith. This one sentence is clearly serious, but it belongs to an otherwise rather lighthearted meditation (on platitudes); and it is loose — distinctly *décousu*. Notice again the effect of a lengthy concluding participial phrase.

Then the pride in the British Constitution and British Freedom, which comes over me when I see, even in the distance, the Towers of Westminster Palace — that Mother of Parliaments — it is not much comfort that this should be chastened, as I walk down the Embankment, by the sight of Cleopatra's Needle, and the Thought that it will no doubt witness the Fall of the British, as it has of other Empires, remaining to point its Moral, as old as Egypt, to Antipodeans musing on the dilapidated bridges.[20]

This writer is one of the few in our century who has really known how to take his time. Let me quote the remainder of this short piece.

I am sometimes afraid of finding that there is a moral for everything; that the whole great frame of the Universe has a key, like a box; has been contrived and set going by a well-meaning but humdrum Eighteenth-century Creator. It would be a kind of Hell, surely, a world in which everything could be at once explained, shown to be obvious and useful. I am sated with Lesson and Allegory, weary of monitory ants, industrious bees, and preaching animals. The benefits of Civilization cloy me. I have seen enough shining of the didactic Sun.

So gazing up on hot summer nights at the London stars, I cool my thoughts with a vision of the giddy, infinite, meaningless waste of Creation, the blazing Suns, the Planets and frozen Moons, all crashing blindly for ever across the void of space.[21]

When the modern essayist decides to bear down on us with a battery of short, sharp statements like those in the middle of the foregoing passage, he feels it virtually necessary to lace them with humor. He ventures opinions rather than laws and does so more in the spirit of play than of the didacticism that Logan Pearsall Smith here deplores. He talks about "monitory ants," "preaching animals," and "the shining of the didactic Sun." Something seems to warn him that the age of serious prophecy is past. When we moderns want to be most serious, we often take the most care to avoid hitting from the shoulder. We beguile. We make apologies and protestations. We wonder, we surmise, we conjecture. We weave a daisy chain. When we hit hard, it is with a bladder on a stick. Here is a characteristic salvo of short, sharp shocks by Arnold Bennett:

Philosophers have explained space. They have not explained time. It is the inexplicable raw material of everything. With it, all is possible; without it, nothing. The supply of time is truly a miracle, an affair genuinely astonishing when one examines it. You wake up in the morning, and lo! your purse is magically filled with twenty-four hours of the unmanufactured tissue of the universe of your life! It is yours. It is the most precious of possessions. A highly singular commodity, showered upon you in a manner as singular as the commodity itself!

For remark! No one can take it from you. It is unstealable. And no one receives either more or less than you receive.

Talk about an ideal democracy! In the realm of time there is no aristocracy of wealth, and no aristocracy of intellect. Genius is never rewarded by even an extra hour a day. And there is no punishment . . .[22]

And here, once more, is Robert Louis Stevenson hammering away almost as hard and quite as gaily:

The air of the fireside withers out all the fine wildings of the husband's heart. He is so comfortable and happy that he begins to prefer comfort and happiness to everything else on earth, his wife included. Yesterday he would have shared his last shilling; to-day "his first duty is to his family," and is fulfilled in large measure by laying down vintages and husbanding the health of an invaluable parent. Twenty years ago this man was equally capable of crime or heroism; now he is fit for neither; you will not wake him. It is not for nothing that Don Quixote was a bachelor and Marcus Aurelius married ill.[23]

The tone of voice of these writers is, of course, none other than that of Charles Lamb:

Ten to one he [a suckling pig] would have proved a glutton, a sloven, an obstinate, disagreeable animal — wallowing in all manner of filthy conversation — from these sins he is happily snatched away —
> Ere sin could blight, or sorrow fade,
> Death came with timely care —
his memory is odoriferous — no clown curseth, while his stomach half rejecteth, the rank bacon — no coalheaver bolteth him in reeking sausages — he hath a fair sepulchre in the grateful stomach of the judicious epicure — and for such a tomb might be content to die.[24]

Lamb, we might say, standardized the tradition that humor is the way of independence for the latter-day prophet. Here are some illuminating comments on him by Gilbert Norwood, in the master's own manner:

He cherished a whimsical affection for Elizabethan playwrights, some of them rubbish; and (as one result) arid nincompoops are obtaining doctorates for research into the "outlook," "Italian Sources," and the like, of such wretches as Glapthorne and Shakerley Marmion, whose cleverly constructed name is his only asset.

Poor Lamb's at first unfashionable hobby has become a stamping ground for people who, were he alive now, would despise him for reading Longfellow and Hannah More.[25]

THE PROPHETIC STYLE

I think it can be said that authentic prophecy was first heard in English in the late Renaissance. The pre-Renaissance pulpit, wherein preachers denouncing sin had doubtless been doing so more or less in the manner of Jeremiah or Ezekiel from the earliest times, is no real exception, for it does not take a prophet to echo prophets of the past. The medieval pulpit, though, along with the text of the Bible itself, may be supposed to have helped prepare the way for the Renaissance prophets by accustoming people's ears to the oracular tone of voice. The main literary influence, however, as Croll has made amply clear, was the literature of ancient Stoicism; though here again, in view of the extensive common ground between Stoic and Christian doctrine, the Church must be allowed to have done much, albeit unwittingly, to predispose the neo-Stoics — Juste Lipse, Marc Antoine Muret, Bacon, and others — to respond with enthusiasm to their Seneca, Tacitus, Epictetus, and Marcus Aurelius.

There is no telling why the new prophets appeared when they did and not earlier or later. All we can do is consider that the political turbulence of the age and the ferocity with which men of inquiring mind were being hunted and harried by guardians of tradition were bound to lend peculiar attraction to a philosophy forged in not dissimilar ancient conditions and strongly expressive of intellectual independence and indifference to fortune.

Ciceronian rhetoric, though but a century earlier still a novelty, had, like Aristotelian logic in the days of Scholasticism, soon passed from a fashion into a rigid standard. It became so directly associated with religious orthodoxy that a writer's faith could be called in question if his prose style betrayed the guiding light of any other authority.[26] Prose style, indeed, is perhaps the most visibly revolutionary phase of the influence of Stoic literature in the sixteenth century, for much of this influence was gradual and unobtrusive. Seneca had been widely read in the Middle Ages, and no principle was more stressed by the medieval Church than contempt for the world. The *De Constantia* of Juste Lipse recalls much of the thought common to Seneca and St. Paul, and its tone of voice, like that of the verse epistles of the wise and gentle poet Samuel Daniel, a veritable summary of Stoic doctrine, implies no rebellious or revolutionary intent.

Lipse and Daniel reflect the serene rather than the defiant side of Stoicism. They do not teach hope, but peace of mind in a precarious world, as Seneca did under Nero.

During the English Civil War and Commonwealth, voices of two very different kinds spoke in prose with distinction. Parliamentary leaders like Eliot, Pym, and Cromwell, whose cause had been indebted earlier to many a moralist of euphuistic bent and many a tumbling pamphlet, now deliberating upon practical issues of great urgency, spoke with an eloquence and polish worthy of Cicero himself. The gloomy doctrines of election and predestination, common to Puritan and Stoic philosophy, seem not to have had the slightest enervating effect upon the vigor of these men. But from the losing side came a quite different tune. Here were men ruminating, in the prophetic, essayistic vein, upon anything and everything except current affairs. Burton, Browne, Sir Thomas Urquhart, Fuller, and Cowley were all good but ineffectual Royalists, and seem, by comparison with the Parliament men, so many amiable, fluent, half-Shandean antiquarians.

The eighteenth century was much more an age of purpose and discipline than of surrender or resignation, and to that extent could be called optimistic. It produced some pessimistic writing and a few pieces of rare eccentricity (what could be queerer than *The Life and Opinions of John Buncle?*); but the Civil War and intellectual chaos of the seventeenth century were long past, and the characteristic prose of the new age, apart from fiction, was the tactful expository prose of the periodicals. In the reasonableness and orderly workmanship of this literature we sense a firm conviction that everyday life is worth living, as we do not in the uncentered, visionary, groping, variously somber and facetious, often brilliant but often messy prose of the pre-Restoration writers.

In the Romantic Revival the resurgence of the earlier essay style appears to be simply a phase of the general revival of interest in all things pre-Augustan. The "humours" of the seventeenth-century prosemen, their outworn erudition, their love of strange words, their delight in paradox and pun, and their unbuttoned syntax can all be illustrated first and last from the prose of Lamb, Southey, Hazlitt, and Coleridge, by comparison with which the elegant periodical essays of the Addisonian tradition read more like miniature treatises than like essays of the authentic, prophetic genus.

But a prophet arose in their midst whom, in spite of his undeniable stature, or rather because of it, it is hard to forgive when he forgets his manners. The example of his more complacent utterances comes to mind inevitably as we read certain contemporary and later writers in the oracular vein, whether or not he was an influence upon them — men who have all had enthusiastic admirers, but no general popularity, almost certainly because their manner has seemed too much like an unfriendly dare or *defi*.

In many of Carlyle's paragraphs he jumps treacherously from one type of style to another, as if it were beneath him to submit to any one set of conventions. For example:

O reader, I say not who are Belial's elect. This poor amphibious Pope too gives loaves to the Poor; has in him more good latent than he is himself aware of. His poor Jesuits, in the late Italian Cholera, were, with a few German Doctors, the only creatures whom dastard terror had not driven mad: they descended fearless into all gulfs and bedlams; watched over the pillow of the dying, with help, with counsel and hope; shone as luminous fixed stars, when all else had gone out in chaotic night: honour to them! This poor Pope, — who knows what good is in him? In a Time otherwise too prone to forget, he keeps up the mournfulest ghastly memorial of the Highest, Blessedest, which once was; which, in new fit forms, will again partly have to be. Is he not as a perpetual death's-head and cross-bones, with their *Resurgam*, on the grave of a Universal Heroism, — grave of a Christianity? Such Noblenesses, purchased by the world's best heart's-blood, must not be lost; we cannot afford to lose them, in what confusions soever. To all of us the day will come, to a few of us it has already come, when no mortal, with his heart yearning for a "Divine Humility," or other "Highest form of Valour," will need to look for it in death's-heads, but will see it round him in here and there a beautiful living head.

Besides, there is in this poor Pope, and his practice of the Scenic Theory of Worship, a frankness which I rather honour. . . .[27]

Here is a writer determined to force himself, instead of his subject, upon our attention. How can we be impressed with the "Divine" theme of "Humility" when its expounder puts on such a parade of mannerism, bad taste, and general condescension? It is impertinent enough for him to speak of "This poor Pope" and deign to allow in him "a frankness which I rather honour"; but his opening protestation is worse, for though it expresses restraint, the form of it implies that he could indeed say "who are Belial's elect" if he chose to do so. And certain other traits of expression, which, because habitual with him in all of his later writings, further tend to put forward himself instead of his subject are easy to spot: his constant use of appositives; a sometimes queer, nonchalant word order (e.g., "in here and there a beautiful living head"); and a Teutonic love of abstract words ("Highest, Blessedest"; "Noblenesses"; etc.).

Carlyle as a highly individual, even eccentric and highhanded stylist is more or less matched by three men whose names have often been linked with his in one connection or another: Emerson, Meredith, and, in poetry, Browning. Though they were not all, like Carlyle, positively hero-worshippers, all were fascinated by men in great place, whether true heroes or not. Emerson, though a citizen of a free commonwealth, was devoted to the idea of a natural aristocracy and the ideal of the self-made man; and so were Browning and Meredith. None of the three appears like a Stoic prophet of doom; quite the contrary. All could be called optimists. Browning and Meredith delighted to portray capricious tyrants, and both are famous obscurantists. Browning's portraits of his Renaissance dukes and bishops, and Meredith's of his egoists of the Victorian feudal order, are ironical, but the irony could almost be mistaken for cynicism. Each seems to say, let us see how near we can come to a completely uncritical view of these rascals.

As stylists, all three, along with Carlyle, look like ancestors of a school of novelists who have flourished within living memory. I see the style of these latter as a type, and am fain to characterize it as the narrative counterpart of the essentially non-narrative prophetic style we have been describing. To illustrate, I will quote in order, with no more than a passing comment or two, from Meredith, Wyndham Lewis, and James Joyce.

Here, first, is a passage from Meredith's *Diana of the Crossways*

(1885) — not too obscure, perhaps, but clearly meant, as Meredith himself might say, to be Mandarin to the vulgar:

Her [Diana's] thought of the gentleman was of a brilliant young charioteer in the ruck of the race, watchful for his chance to push to the front; and she could have said that a dubious consort might spoil a promising career. It flattered her to think that she sometimes prompted him, sometimes illumined. He repeated sentences she had spoken. — "I shall be better able to describe Mr. Dacier when you and I sit together, my Emmy, and a stroke here and there completes the painting. Set descriptions are good for puppets. Living men and women are too various in the mixture fashioning them — even the 'external presentment' — to be livingly rendered in a formal sketch. I may tell you his eyes are pale blue, his features regular, his hair silky, brownish, his legs long, his head rather stooping (only the head), his mouth commonly closed; these are the facts, and you have seen much the same in a nursery doll. Such literary craft is of the nursery. So with landscapes. The art of the pen (we write on darkness) is to rouse the inward vision, instead of labouring with a Drop-scene brush, as if it were to the eye; because our flying minds cannot contain a protracted description. That is why the poets, who spring imagination with a word or a phrase, paint lasting pictures. The Shakespearian, the Dantesque, are in a line, two at most. He lends an attentive ear when I speak, agrees or has a quaint pucker of the eyebrows dissenting inwardly. He lacks mental liveliness — cheerfulness, I should say, and is thankful to have it imparted. One suspects he would be a dull domestic companion. He has a veritable thirst for hopeful views of the world, and no spiritual distillery of his own. He leans to depression. Why! The broken reed you call your Tony carries a cargo, all of her manufacture — she reeks of secret stills; and here is a young man — a sapling oak — inclined to droop. His nature has an air of imploring me *que je l'arrose!* I begin to perform Mrs. Dr. Pangloss on purpose to brighten him — the mind, the views. He is not altogether deficient in conversational gaiety, and he shines in exercise. But the world is a poor old ball bounding down a hill — to an Irish melody in the evening generally, by request. So far of Mr. Percy Dacier, of whom I have some hopes — distant, perhaps delusive — that he may be of use to our cause. He listens. It is an auspicious commencement."[28]

We seem to see in Meredith, and still more clearly in Wyndham Lewis and the later James Joyce, something of the attitude noted in Gertrude Stein by Thornton Wilder: "Miss Stein's theory of the audience insists . . . that the richest rewards for the reader have come from those works in which the authors admitted no consideration of an audience into their creating mind."[29] Here is Wyndham Lewis:

He laughs, clearing up the atmosphere. Exit Fathers like a cohort of witches, turning tail at sight of the bristling righteous phalanx of incestuous masculine matrons, with hittite profiles, hanging out like hatchets just clear of the chest, Eton-cropped, short stout necks firmly anchored in asthmatic lungs, with single eyeglasses, and ten diamond corking-pins representing the decaceraphorous beast of the deliverance. They guard the child-herds. Revolutionary cockades bouquet'd with spatulate figleaves, symbolic of absolute divorce anti-family son-love and purple passion, dissimulate their abdominal nudity. Pulley barks fiercely: he is the gelded herd-dog. He barks at the heels of the Fathers, bearded despotic but now despatched.[30]

And here is perhaps the boldest experiment in style ever attempted, *Finnegans Wake*:

Evidentament he has failed as tiercely as the deuce before for she is wearing none of the three. And quite as patently there is a hole in the ballet trough which the rest fell out. Because to explain why the residue is, was, or will not be, according to the eighth axiom, proceeded with, namely, since ever apart that gossuan duad, so sure as their's a patch on a pomelo, this yam ham in never live could, the shifting about of the lassies, the tug of love of their lads ending with a great deal of merriment, hoots, screams, scarf drill, cap fecking, ejaculations of aurinos, reechoable mirthpeals and general thumbtonosery (Myama's a yaung yaung cauntry), one must reckon with the sudden and gigantesquesque appearance unwithstandable as a general election in Barnado's bearskin amongst the brawlmiddle of this village childergarten of the largely longsuffering laird of Lucanhof.[31]

Will mature reflection allow the various writings we have been sampling to constitute a genuine or significant category? I am persuaded that it will. In all of them, by whatever names we designate their several species, the writer speaks, whether seriously, half-seriously, or only for a lark, as if without responsibility to any person, law, or other identifiable check upon his freedom. If he defers to any check, it was his choice, had he pleased — such is the implication of his style — to have done otherwise. The test of the greatness of a great idea is experience and logical analysis; but its birth is always a mystery, and no wonder that the first expression given it should often be a flat, unsupported assertion. Nor any wonder that the authority of the great, proven aphorisms should have tempted many a nobody to try on the prophetic mantle and make an appearance in it comparable to that of small children at make-believe games in grown-ups' clothes. Our genre has been the vehicle of scriptural doctrine; of much grave and brilliant secular comment, both ancient and modern, on life and manners; of much ingenious and quaint, often playful speculation; and the vehicle of much odious because pretentious and perverse laying down of law. Fiction, too, even fiction, commonly the most perspicuous of all reading matter, has now and then appeared in the darker kind of prophetic guise, warning away the everyday reader, while offering a lively chase to the adventurous.

THE INDENTURE STYLE

Legal Documents · Private Formal Messages

Le utility del chose excusera le noisomeness del stink.
— From an English court's
finding in an old law case.

M Y TITLE refers to the style traditional in the strict legal instrument and various kindred kinds of writing.

When it first occurred to me to look into the rationale and history of this very distinctive style, I supposed, considering the central part it plays in the world of affairs, the staggering mass of the handwritten and printed matter that has been and is daily being composed in it, not to mention its influence off and on in belles-lettres, that lawyers or legal librarians could direct me at once to a full literature on the subject. To my surprise, I found that none of my consultants could name so much as a single book or article addressed directly to my problem.

Certain earmarks of the style and its characteristic flavor are perfectly familiar to everybody, even persons of no formal education, as, for example, Joel Chandler Harris's Uncle Remus. In Uncle Remus's tale of the Great Deluge, he tells how all the animals gather to hold an assembly and how, during the proceedings, the elephant "tromples" one of the crawfishes. "De udder crawfishes got mighty mad," he says, "en dey sorter swarmed tergedder and draw'd up a kinder peramble wid some wharfo'es in it, en read her out in de 'sembly." [1] Lawyers know how to write it; men of letters know how to make fun of it; and professors of "diplomatic" and the history of rhetoric supply a wealth of information about drafting in the Middle Ages and the training of the scrivener. The writers on "diplomatic" are the most helpful, but the object of their attention is more the what of the style than the why of it, and they say nothing of its influence outside the scrivener's workshop.

The indenture style is very formal, for it expresses or contemplates law, and impersonal, answering to the impersonal position of all parties that any instrument may concern, which is that of their status. Ralph or Roger becomes the deponent or the plaintiff, the lessee, the grantor, the accused, the beneficiary, the testator, the court, or such a matter.

Its elevated air is the literary counterpart of the ostentatious getup of the physical document. The prose is massive and difficult. It is difficult because it aims at the last degree of precision, and all the more so because of the age-old fondness of draftsmen for cluttering up their documents with superfluities. "Superfluities," though, may not be quite the right word, for it is obvious that an instrument is meant to look imposing, and whatever swells its mere bulk, however objectionable otherwise, is of some effect to this end.

Most instruments, as we know, describe what seems more like a static position than the movement we associate with narrative discourse, but every instrument is, in fact, a narrative: it "narrates" the act by which the author (single or plural) commits himself, by means of his seal and signature, to the pledge, executive order, petition, or other business in hand.

The act is a single, theoretically instantaneous act. It would seem, though I have not met this explanation in any authority, that it is the single character of the act that explains the practice, now less general than it used to be, but still common, of crowding the whole text of an instrument into a single, sometimes painfully long-winded sentence, the sentence being traditionally regarded by grammarians as the most strictly unified expression of a single, complete idea. The sentence is often compound as well as complex, and its several predications often only loosely bound together, yet the convention is usually clear that we are not to take these predications as independent units, but as parts of a single, compound whole. Perhaps it is feared that separate sentences could be taken out of context more easily than parts of one sentence and their meaning thus misread.

There is internal evidence for the convention in most documents, and external evidence in the expressed attitude the courts have taken toward punctuation when punctuation taken at face value might yield a different meaning from that of the same text unpunctuated.

In many a text of the traditional kind containing two or more complete predications, these will be separated with full stops, and the first word after each stop capitalized; but each predication after a stop will be found to begin with a conjunction (commonly "and," "and further," or "and likewise"); though to make sure that there shall be no misunderstanding of the scope of the new predication, various formulas (appellatives, and the like) are commonly repeated from previous predications, as in the following clause from the Charter of Massachusetts Bay (1629), wherein I have italicized the repeated elements: "And further *our Will and Pleasure* is, and Wee doe hereby *for Vs, our Heires and Successors*, ordeyne and declare, and graunte to *the saide Governor and Company, and their Successors* . . ." [2]

Decisive proof that the mark of the full stop followed by a capitalized word is not meant to be taken at face value is the fact that the capitalized word often introduces not a new, complete predication but a sentence member that cannot be read as syntactically independent of what precedes. Thus we find in the same Charter: "to be appointed to fishe therein. Provided alwayes, That yf the said landes"; and again, "therein conteyned to the contrarie notwithstanding. To have and hould, possesse and enioy the said partes of New England . . ." [3]

And the courts are explicit:

Punctuation is a most fallible standard by which to interpret a writing; it may be resorted to when all other means fail, but the court will first ascertain the meaning from the four corners of the instrument; 11 Pet. 64.

More particularly (italics mine),

In construing deeds, it is said that no regard is to be had to punctuation, and although stops are sometimes used, they are not to be regarded in the construction of the instrument; 3 Washb. R.P. 397. See 21 W. Va. 707. *Punctuation is not allowed to throw light on printed statutes in England*; 24 Beav. 330.

In an act of Parliament there are no such things as brackets, any more than there are such things as stops; 24 Q.B.D. 478.

. . . Punctuation may be *considered* in determining the meaning of a contract, when it is doubtful; 138 U.S.I.

Where a comma after a word in a statute, if any force were attached to it, would give the section containing it broader scope than it would otherwise have, it was held that that circumstance should not have a controlling influence. Punctuation is no part of the statute; 105 U.S. 77; in construing statutes, courts will disregard punctuation; or, if need be, repunctuate, to render the true meaning of the statute; 16 Ohio St. 432, approved in 105 U.S. 77; also 65 Pa. 311; 9 Gray 385.

Lord St. Leonards said; "In wills and deeds you do not ordinarily find any stops; but the court reads them as if they were properly punctuated;" 2 Dr. & War. 98.

Judges in the later cases have been influenced in construing wills by the punctuation of the original document; 2 M. & G. 679; 26 Beav. 81; 1 Phila. 528; 17 Beav. 589; 24 L.J. Ch. 523; but see 1. Mer. 651, where Sir William Grant refused to resort to punctuation as an aid to construction. See also 25 Barb. 405; 16 Can L.J. 183.[4]

Sufficient reasons for the distrust of punctuation, though I have not seen them stated, would seem to be the danger that punctuation marks, being small, could be confused with accidental blots of ink or defects in the paper and easier for the dishonest to forge or erase, and that in comparison with other conventions of grammar, those of punctuation have never been very stable. In a modern instrument made up of separate numbered sentences for its several sections, the numbers serve for stops; but draftsmen are still instructed to make their meaning clear without depending on punctuation marks.

The interesting question immediately arises as to how the rule affects the style of composition, and on this the only comment I have noticed is the one quoted above, that there are no such things as brackets (presumably meaning also parentheses) or stops in an act of Parliament. To this, one may add that extra care in the wording becomes necessary to distinguish between restrictive and nonrestrictive clauses and that the repetitiousness I have mentioned becomes almost inevitable, though behind this other causes may be suspected, as we shall see. For the moment we may simply notice that, given the old ideal of making a single sentence contain the whole act, the easy way to clarity in the absence of punctuation (though not necessarily to perspicuity, much less to elegance) is repetitiousness, just as the easy way to the inclusion of a large amount of content in a single sentence is loose compounding.

Indenture prose has always tended, and probably always will, to be more copious than other kinds. Not only is it typically swelled with the reiteration of workaday expressions, but any typical act, say a will or a contract, must contemplate an enormous range and variety of possible contingencies, and these require to be carefully set forth. General expressions can, of course, cover wide areas of meaning, but the tendency of draftsmen has been, as we all know, to distrust general language and therefore to spell out all foreseeable applications of any act in full. Modern authorities have warned against the enumeration of particulars, on the ground that "It is almost impossible to make the enumeration exhaustive, and accidental omission may be construed as implying deliberate exclusion, in accordance with the canon 'Expressio unius est exclusio alterius' "; but they are reconciled to the sacrifice of brevity where clarity is otherwise unattainable.[5]

Long-windedness, as opposed to prolixity, can, properly speaking, only be a feature of the single sentence and has reference not to its mere length, though it involves length, but to the amount and complexity of the thought that the reader must hold in suspension as he goes forward. A long-winded sentence is one in which the sense remains unresolved for a long stretch. Prolixity can aggravate long-windedness, but (as Jeremy Bentham explains) the essence of the long-winded sentence is the inclusion in it of matter that ought to be distributed among two or perhaps several sentences.[6] A sentence, however, can be lengthened almost indefinitely by compounding without presenting this kind of difficulty; and the fact that draftsmen commonly compound the sentence in any long document and invite a stop-and-go reading by providing for the eye numerous full stops (even while maintaining with their connective words the fiction of the whole text as one sentence) presumably indicates that they are mindful of both their own and the reader's convenience.

But why should tradition have sanctioned, as it did long ago, a prolixity exaggerated far beyond what anybody could think convenient for either writer or reader?[7] I have heard it said in legal circles, as if it were a commonplace to be taken for granted, that the older prolixity is accountable simply to the fact that draftsmen used to be paid by the page.[8] This explanation implies draftsmen accorded a free hand by their employers, and no doubt they were allowed a maximum of freedom when, as commonly in the Middle Ages, the employer, though a potentate and man of substance, was often illiterate, and again in the Renaissance and subsequently when, though literacy had now become general in the governing classes, law had been developed into a science too complicated for laymen to dare tinker with prose involving its technicalities.

When Jeremy Bentham, disgusted with the prolixity of the eighteenth-century statutes, urged that drafting should be done in a more succinct style, the legal profession would not listen to him. He could only conclude that their reason for writing a prose that nobody but they could read was to ensure themselves steady and lucrative business.[9]

No doubt we must allow for all of these various considerations: first of all, the generic requirements of fulness and precision in a kind of discourse intended to exhibit the strictest unity yet without the help of punctuation, and, secondarily, divers but cooperating motives in the scriveners' profession — intellectual laziness, pedantry, self-interest, and, finally, the laudable desire to make sure that their documents should correspond in weight to the majesty of the law that they state or contemplate, even if only in the crude weight of swollen bulk. This last consideration is not suggested by any of the authorities I have consulted, perhaps because they have thought it sufficiently obvious to be taken for granted, though not many of them are given to looking for high-mindedness in scriveners. I take it to be obvious, and something we should associate in our minds with all of the other ways in which documents are made to look imposing.

The diction of the prose traditional in legal instruments runs, at one extreme, to pompous generality, notably in salutations and pre-ambles, and at the other to technical terms that we seldom, if ever, meet elsewhere. Since law goes by precedent, these technical terms often have an archaic flavor. Many otherwise archaic words have come to stand for concepts that courts have defined with a good deal of precision, and such words have therefore become permanent technical terms in legal business. Much of the jargon in the English-speaking countries naturally derives from Latin and French. As to Latin, not only was it from Rome that all the northern peoples first learned the arts of codifying their native laws and making new ones and much about legal administration, but, more particularly, Latin, at the time of the Norman Conquest, "was the language of such legal documents as the Normans knew" and was also at that time already "the language of the English charters or land-books." [10] And it became in addition, and remained until as late as 1731 "the language of our voluminous official and judicial records." French early became the language of the privy seal, of the Parliament rolls and statute rolls, and of pleading; the decisive year, according to Pollock and Maitland, being, not 1066 but 1166, the year of "the assize of novel disseisin . . . [the year when] the decree went forth which gave to every man dispossessed of his freehold a remedy to be sought in a royal court, a French-speaking court." Thus our jar-gon includes such Latin terms as *mittimus, nolle prosequi, assumpsit,* and *habeas corpus,* and such French ones as *assize, disseisin, tort, trover,* and *cestuy que trust* — Pollock and Maitland mention some seventy examples, and could have mentioned plenty more — beside a very few native English words, some, though technical, being of frequent occurrence in everyday talk, like *deed, theft,* and *man-slaughter,* others seldom met outside of legal instruments, like *free-hold* and *siblings.*

But it is not only technical terms that give legal diction its archaic character. In many documents of the present day we find such dis-tinctly dated but in no sense technical forms as the *-th* third person of verbs, the *do-*, *did-* instead of the uncompounded present and past tenses ("The lessor hath let, leased, and demised"; "The lessor doth, further irrevocably authorize the lessee"), archaic past participles like "holden" for "held" ("our said district court to be holden at ————"), and the pronoun "ye" ("Now know ye that we the underwriters do hereby bind ourselves . . .").[11] Here is archaism whose function is purely aesthetic. The layman, moreover, cannot fail to feel an element of mystery in the occurrence of perfectly familiar words to express meanings that he can see from the way the words are used are not their common meanings. In ordinary usage one cannot "sell" an object to somebody and at the same time "give" it to him; but in a common form of conveyance the author agrees to "give, grant, bargain, sell and confirm" to the other party a piece of real estate.

And of course the legal French used for reporting court cases in England long after French had gone out of use in the country at large — at least as late as the reign of Charles I, and, for all I know later still — provides illustrations of the archaizing tendency that read like caricatures, such as the epigraph of the present chapter. Most lawyers, I suppose, have at one time or another encountered this strange lingo, but it is less generally known to laymen, and I trust I shall be forgiven if I take space to retail a couple of further remarkable examples:

Coke: Ceo n'est d'estre fait nisi request soit fait, come si jeo soie oblige a paier un somme al jour certein sur request ceo n'est ascun dutie devant request (R. [i.e., reporter]. Quaere ceo car Haughton semble a disallower ceo, car il shake son capit al ceo).

Richardson, ch. Just. de C. Banc al assizes at Salisbury in Summer 1631. fuit assault per prisoner la condemne pur felony que puis son condemnation ject un Brickbat a le dit Justice que narrowly mist, & pur ceo immediately fuit Indictment drawn per Noy envers le prisonner, & son dexter manus ampute & fix al Gibbet sur que luy mesme immediatement hange in presence de Court.[12]

The style runs, moreover, to poetry — of idea as well as of diction — not only in monumental documents like Magna Carta and the Declaration of Independence, but also in papers executed daily in the little business affairs of Main Street. Draftsmen are fond of stressing the ultimate reaches of a legal position, and all but take our breath away when, in a run-of-the-mill business instrument, they look back to the creation, or forward to eternity. A form of release currently employed cancels liabilities incurred on a given account since "the beginning of the world"; so-called "ground leases" in the state of Vermont — and no doubt elsewhere — afford the lessee the use of the property "while grass grows and water runs"; and if Jones buys an acre of land from Smith, Smith deeds it to him, his heirs, and assigns "forever." [13]

ORIGINS OF THE STYLE

The style first appears in two ancient types of document: first, the ancient letter transmitting governmental directives, military orders, and the various messages exchanged between potentates that we now call "foreign correspondence"; and, second, the type of memorandum in the third person that came into use in ancient Rome to record transactions between parties present in person.

No use of written language appears to be older than that of providing a vehicle for official messages. Writing, we are told, originated as, and long remained, a highly specialized craft, and seems to have been at first a convenience available only to persons in high place, such as could afford to employ professional scribes. It has been noticed that King David, the first letter writer mentioned in the Old Testament, sent his command to Joab concerning Uriah the Hittite in writing, but that Joab replied by means of an oral message (2 Samuel xi.14, 18ff). Few of the surviving documents of antiquity are older than those discovered at Tell el Amarna in Egypt, which are all letters of about the middle of the second millennium B.C., indited on clay tablets and addressed to the Pharaoh by various local princes in Palestine in a language said to resemble the Hebrew of the Old Testament.

As in medieval diplomatic letters, so in these of the Tell el Amarna collection, the salutation is elaborate and more or less strictly conventionalized with respect to the relative rank of addressee and author. Different writers of a given rank adhere with only minor variations to one formula for a given rank of addressee. There is no attempt to crowd the whole message into one sentence, but the writer is never in a hurry; rather, he is intent above all things upon a scrupulous observance of those proprieties that have always been exigent in public business and upon precision in stating material facts. Here are two samples:

To *Amenophis III*, the Great King, King of *Egypt*, my brother, my kinsman whom I love, and who loves me, by letter thus *Tusratta*, the Great King, King of *Mitani*, thy brother, thy kinsman who also loves thee. I am at peace. Peace be to thee. To thy house, thy wives, thy sons, thy lords, thy terrible army, thy horses, thy chariots, and in thy land, be much peace.

Since your forefathers were friendly with my forefathers, thou therefore wast very greatly friendly with my father. So you love me: we are zealous friends. Ten times more you increase it than to my father. The heavenly Gods shall decree that we shall be friends. May *Rimmon* my God, and *Amanu*, so pronounce, even forever.

And so my brother sent *Mani* his envoy. This indeed my brother (said) "Does not my brother's heart desire that thy daughter (be) the wife of my young son — as a princess of *Egypt*" and I spoke as to my intention about it; and my brother desiring that she should be ready for *Mani*, and to show her, so he beheld her, and praised her much. And may they lead her in peace into the land of my brother. May *Istar* and *Amanu* make her agreeable to my brother's heart. . . .

Now as to the gifts for my brother: I have sent as my brother's gifts a quantity of solid gold, and precious stones: (its value?) includes the amount of twenty precious stones, and nineteen pieces of gold. The weight of precious stones and gold remaining includes the amount of forty-two precious stones and twenty pieces of gold *Zusas* of Istar: (this is) the weight of precious stones and gold remaining; and ten yoke of horses, and ten chariots, with all that belongs to them, and thirty female slaves.[14]

Tusratta evidently wrote as the equal of his correspondent. The following quotation is a letter to the same Egyptian king from a tributary chief acknowledging a military order. The first writer sent "peace"; this one bows seven times on his face.

To the king my Lord by letter thus Artabania, chief of the city of Ziribasani, thy servant. At the feet of the King my Lord seven times, on my face, seven times I bow. Behold a message to me to speed to meet the Egyptian soldiers. And who am I but a dog only, and shall

I not march? Behold me, with my soldiers and my chariots meeting the Egyptian soldiers at the place which the King my Lord speaks [of].[15]

The existence of ancient archives in various parts of the Mediterranean and Near Eastern world illustrates the early and wide recognition of what a convenient vehicle and record writing provides for important messages. Nor need we doubt that precautions were taken from the beginning to guard against forgery. The traditional precaution provided by the writer's seal had obviously long since been standard when it proved insufficient for its purpose in the story of Jezebel, who wrote "letters in Ahab's name and sealed them with his seal" (1 Kings xxi.8). Indeed, seals as a means of identifying property (wine jars, and the like) are thought to be considerably older than the alphabet.[16]

The indenture style has been, of course, that of statutes as well as other instruments throughout the history of statute law, as we should expect; and the negative fact is worth our notice in passing that we do *not* find significant anticipations of the style in surviving texts of primitive laws such as the Babylonian Laws of Hammurabi (of the twentieth century B.C.), the Roman Laws of the Twelve Tables (B.C. 451–450),[17] or the Anglo-Saxon Dooms of Aethelbert of Kent (ca. A.D. 600).[18] One might mention at most the very general feature of their impersonality and, in the last named, what has been called a kind of embellishment (each doom is composed in a kind of alliterative verse essentially the same as that of the contemporary heroic poetry).[19]

Classical Greek and Roman instruments illustrate the same clarity that is evident in other kinds of classical prose, and more particularly a new ability to handle long, complex sentences. The writing could even be called elegant, though it is seldom altogether free from that repetition of workaday words and phrases that seems to be generic to the draftsman's art, as in the following passage from the Municipal Law of Julius Caesar:

With regard to those streets which are or shall be in the city of Rome or within a radius of one mile from the city of Rome, — wherever this zone shall be continually built up, — the owner of any building before which any such street shall run, shall maintain the same to the satisfaction of the aedile, to whom this part of the city shall have been assigned in accordance with this law; and that aedile shall see to it that all persons, before whose buildings any streets run, which they shall be obliged by this law severally to maintain, shall severally maintain the same to his satisfaction; and he shall see to it that no water remains standing in any such place which would hinder the public from the convenient use of the street.

The curule aediles and plebeian aediles who are now in office, and whoever after the passing of this law shall have been made or created aediles or shall have entered upon this office, shall, within the next five days after they shall have been elected or shall have entered upon this office, decide . . . etc. . . . etc.[20]

General considerations suggest that we should probably attribute the perfection of the practical side of medieval and modern drafting mainly to the Greeks and Romans, and mainly to Asiatic influence the ceremonious, ornamental side that has been its increasingly conspicuous mark since documents came into wide use with the rise of the legal profession in the late Middle Ages.

To the Romans, moreover, we must attribute in particular the invention of a very distinct form of legal document, namely the memorandum of the kind of transaction that takes place between parties physically present. The distinctive feature of it is that these parties, whom we should now call the authors (i.e., those who authorize the writing), appear in the third person, the implication being that the record is written from the point of view of an onlooker.

In the earliest times, says Sir Henry Maine, "There seems to have been one solemn ceremonial . . . for all solemn transactions, and its name at Rome appears to have been *nexum*."[21] It seems to have been an act of exchange, a surrender of something valuable by one party to another in return for value received. For a long period the only acts of unofficial people that required public notice or certification were mancipation or sale, adoption, marriage (long recognized as a form of adoption), somewhat later the will or testament (like adoption, long recognized as a form of sale), and, finally, the contract.[22]

Before writing came into use, the means of public certification of the transaction was the presence and attention of a large number of witnesses, who were naturally expected to remember all the details of the transaction.

The antiquity of enacted ritual of one kind or another in all societies, the comparatively late invention of the art of writing, and the measure of formality still observed in public proceedings like the installation of magistrates, the conferring of academic degrees and military commissions, and marriage, all of which are nevertheless attested by written documents that serve as sufficient legal proof of the events they record, suggest that the earliest use of writing in connection with the Roman ceremonial of mancipation and like transactions must have been tentative and incidental. Such, indeed, it seems to have been. Available evidence has not enabled the authorities to say with any precision when written memoranda of these transactions were first thought of or when they were first accorded probative value. Sir Henry Maine thinks it likely that even the plebeian will, a rather late Roman invention (legalized by the Twelve Tables, B.C. 450), was at first executed only by oral publication in the Comitia Calata, though a memorandum may have been made of its substance to be retained by the testator.[23] Bresslau, having distinguished between the kind of document serving merely to recall a legal *fait accompli* (the mere Beweisurkunde) and the kind setting forth and designed to provide proof of an act brought to completion only by the issuance of the document itself (the dispositive kind), remarks that the oldest Roman law knew only the former, and knew it only in the form of plain statements of witnesses.[24]

It is surprising to learn that as late as the reign of Nero a buyer of goods at auction, having paid for them, *himself* writes a statement of the fact and thinks the document worth filing, instead, it seems, of obtaining a proper receipt from the seller. Such a document could obviously have no more probative force than a modern entry in a payor's account book, and its existence seems all the more strange when we find that by this time proper receipts are in use. These belong to a broad classification of instruments known as *chirographa*, since their authenticity depends on the handwriting. The more effective character of the chirographum argues it a later invention than the other type of memorandum, which it is said to have completely supplanted after the third century A.D., at least for certain purposes. The party who receives the document for his files is the one whose interest needs protection, and the writer is the party, or a proxy of the party, whose affirmation gives it.

Chirographa have the special interest of illustrating both the objective and subjective styles and a perfectly logical basis for the writer's choice between them. The writer uses the first person normally, as if he were writing a letter; and the third is used only when the writing is done by a proxy. The subjective chirographum has obviously the character of a letter, except that it contains — originally — no greeting.

At the beginning of Bresslau's great work he says that his central concern is documents clearly purporting to bear witness to legal events and that he will take notice of the business letters of government officials only insofar as their common forms have influenced or been influenced by the more strictly legal kind of instrument. I have looked in vain in his pages (and elsewhere) for any reference to the official Roman business letter as the model of the typical chirographum; but if the latter had a model, what else could it be? It may be that no model was needed for anything so short and simple as the receipts that Bresslau quotes; but the time was not distant when the character of letters was to be recognized throughout the whole category of dispositive instruments. We learn that while the old, legally ineffectual memorandum was passing out of use in early medieval times, the nomenclature of Frankish and Lombardic law preserved — until, says Bresslau, the ninth century — the distinction between it and the dispositive instrument, and that *epistola* was one of three terms applied interchangeably to the latter (the other two being *carta* and *testamentum*). The obsolescent memorandum was called a *notitia, breve,* or *memoratorium.*[25]

If, then, we bear in mind the great antiquity of such extant examples of official correspondence as the Tell el Amarna tablets, the wide use of such correspondence in the classical period (we meet plenty of examples, genuine or simulated, in the classical historians), and the few facts of the history of objective and subjective Roman and early post-Roman instruments that we have just reviewed, the generalization seems warranted that the main tradition of what we now call a legal document or instrument is that of the ancient official or business letter in the first person and that the independently invented Roman memorandum in the third person was in course of time assimilated to this, at least to the extent of being supplied with a greeting and effective authentication, even while retaining, for given purposes, its objective style.

It is of the essence of a letter to be addressed, both explicitly by means of a greeting, or, at least, a vocative, and implicitly, in content and style, to a particular party. It is true, of course, that even the most terse and casual memorandum implies one or more *admonendi*, whether the writer only, or a likely second party (as in a notice to the next caller at the back door, who is expected to be the plumber, that the bell is out of order), or an indefinite public (the label on the bottle of rat poison); but as a type it is less definitely directed. A few modern instruments name no addressee (notes of indebtedness, certain court orders, etc.), but most do, most often by means of a formula contemplating the general public. The commonest formula is probably "To all to whom these presents shall come, [name] send(s) greeting." The limiting expression is plainly not meant as a limit to the number of people who may properly take account of the writing, legal instruments normally being public records in the fullest sense of the word, as we see in the formula sometimes used to open a text not preceded by a greeting strictly so called: "Know all men by these presents . . ." The greeting to "all to whom these presents shall come" is simply a gesture of obeisance to the principle that the residence of law is the people at large. Its all but universal use presumably argues a sense that documents so headed are better oriented in the scheme of things than those without it. A modern letter is incomplete without the author's signature, and some kind of final salutation is usual; but ancient letters ended with a word of salutation only (in Latin, "Vale," "Valete," or the like), the author having already sufficiently identified himself at the beginning ("Cicero Attico sal[utem dicit]").

Further details of the getup of documents between Roman and

modern times can be studied in standard treatises on "diplomatic." Of these details, the use of seals and signatures is of peculiar interest, this being the common modern link between any transaction *in deed* and the same *in law*.

The author's seal, and not his handwriting (as in the early chirographum) or his signature, was the original means by which a letter writer certified his authorship, and it remains today a requirement in many documents, even though the requirement may be met by the use of a cheap gummed wafer bearing no individual mark whatever.[26] The seal is, indeed, wherever called for, the essential certification. It is said to be "a matter of doubt" even today whether, "where a deed is made use of [in conveyancing] . . . signing as well as sealing is absolutely necessary."[27] But this is perhaps not more remarkable than the fact that as late as the reign of Charles II not even a written deed was needed to prove the conveyance of a freeholding, the old ceremonial of livery of seisin in the presence of witnesses (the handing over of a pinch of earth, a door hinge, a key, or such a matter) being alone sufficient to prove the grantee's title.[28]

I mention these curiosities only because they give us a haunting glimpse of a remote past when writing was still a novelty that had yet to prove itself reliable for legal business. And as we reflect upon the ceremonious style of writing that has long been standard in objective documents, as it has always been in official letters, the thought comes to mind that though a memorandum of a ceremonial can be accurate without being written in a ceremonious style, and though the earliest such memoranda were very likely quite bald and unadorned, there would be every reason for the style to reflect the pomp of the ceremonial it records once the document is accorded legal weight.

In the ordinary epistle of former times, as the story of Jezebel's forgery implies, the seal that guaranteed — or seemed to guarantee — its authenticity was that of the author, as today the ordinary guarantee of a letter is the writer's signature; but in the objective type of document, as we learn from Sir Henry Maine, the only seals called for originally were those of the witnesses, since the whole contents of the writing consisted of the witnesses' objective view of the ceremonial enacted by the authors.[29]

Having the strict objectivity of this kind of document in mind, along with what I have called the impersonal position of all parties to the business of all documents, namely their status (that of grantor, grantee, or what not), we may say that impersonality is the soul of the official style. It is the soul of the style because it is the essence of the primary conception of law: law, that is, conceived as custom, therefore as having an existence and authority independent of any extant named lawgiver.[30]

No wonder, then, that a peculiarly authoritative effect is given by instruments of the technically objective kind, as it is also by a narrative like Caesar's *Commentaries* wherein the author plays his leading part in the third person. A narrative statement such as "Caesar crossed the Rhine" or "Caesar sent the tenth legion forward" reads almost like a fact of nature. If Caesar did such and such, and the writer make no reference to himself as "I" or "me," it does not immediately occur to the reader that any "I" or "me" exists to have his veracity called in question. The form of the statement makes it appear to be self-guaranteed.

The weight attaching to impersonal expression of this kind is surely what explains the use of it in many documents that could be composed without inconvenience in the first person — not only official ones like petitions, court orders, and military correspondence, but also quasi-official, private messages like wedding announcements and Harley Street doctors' bills ("Mr. Hamilton presents his compliments and begs to say that his fee for professional services is fifty guineas"). It is perhaps surprising that ancient sovereigns (including Roman emperors) writing formal epistles, and likewise modern kings, popes, and other exalted executives writing not only routine correspondence, but also highly formal charters, patents, decrees, and the like, use the first person. Perhaps it never occurred to the earliest letter writers to affect the third; and to some magistrates the third might seem to betray the weakness of diffidence as to the sufficient prestige of their name and place as expressed in the first person, not to mention the pleasure anyone must be supposed to take in being able to speak with official authority as "I, myself" (the thought occurred to me long ago when I read Woodrow Wilson's war message in 1917, in which I seem to remember, after a preamble, the words "Now therefore I, Woodrow Wilson, President of the United States of America, hereby declare . . .").

The modern authorities on "diplomatic" are much more instructive for our purposes than the rhetoricians who trained draftsmen in the formative period of our style, yet these old rhetoricians are worth a passing glance. In all of their work we see the persistent, overwhelming influence of the classical rhetoric of deliberative oratory, and thus how, in their uncritical subservience to it, they betray themselves true children of their time.

A literature of form-books dates from antiquity. Little is known of the ancient ones,[31] but beginning with the *Liber Diurnus*, of which the oldest manuscript has been dated by de Roziere about 800 A.D. and which contains forms said to have been in use since perhaps the fifth century, a good many handbooks have survived.[32] Many of the late medieval ones expound theory as well as practice, but, so far as my knowledge goes, only in the most perfunctory and irrelevant terms. Subsequent compilers down to, but not including, the twentieth century, have mostly taken theory for granted, and I have been unable to discover anything like a proper draftsman's rhetoric before Jeremy Bentham's *Nomography*. Even this work reached the public only on the eve of the twentieth century, for though Bentham died in 1832, it was not printed until 1893.[33] Today we have a fairly full and systematic rhetoric of drafting, thanks to a new school of writers who have taken up the subject since 1900.

My curiosity about indenture prose was first aroused by a short chapter in C. S. Baldwin's admirable volume, *Medieval Rhetoric and Poetic*,[34] in which he surveys the literature of the formularies and gives a brief digest of one of them, the *Candelabrum* (of the early thirteenth century). He points out, first, the intimate connection of the voluminous letter writing of the Middle Ages with both diplomacy and law, and, second, the extent to which that letter writing was indebted to ancient rhetoric.

He thinks that the classical influence was salutary: in particular, that "of the traditional five parts of ancient rhetoric, *inventio, dispositio,* and *elocutio,* though not *pronuntiatio* and *memoria,* bear directly on letters," and that "immediately adaptable were the five parts of a speech." [35] Perhaps so, in a very general way; but for the composition of strict instruments or diplomatic letters, how much was to be learned from the ancient rules under the head of style (*elocutio*)? What has the wording of a decree, a treaty, or a conveyance to do with the art of persuasion — persuasion, indeed, in spoken discourse?

One of the earliest and most influential of the medieval compilers whose works have survived was Alberic of Monte Cassino, who lived in the eleventh century and wrote three treatises on the art. He was the first to state the rule that an epistle should have five parts and a few other rules and definitions that a long line of successors in various parts of Europe repeat with little or no change, addition, or comment, as one may see by running over the collection of seventeen treatises and parts of treatises reprinted by Rockinger.[36] Defects common to most of them include a too comprehensive announced scope (they commonly pretend to teach the whole art of composition, yet are actually concerned with little except legal and diplomatic discourse), a timid generality in the explanations they offer, mistaken etymologies, a plethora of synonyms for *epistola* and consequent lack of precision in any of them, quaint analogies, pedantic and forced classifications, and an emphasis on the *cursus* that seems excessive and is never explained. Note the following classification in Alberic's *Rationes Dictandi*: "The *narratio* is sometimes 'simplex,' sometimes 'multiplex.' The 'simplex' is a *narratio* in which a single transaction is set forth; the 'multiplex,' one in which several transactions are set forth." [37] A thirteenth-century *Summa Prosarum Dictaminis* equates the whole thing that it calls "the Roman style" with a particular kind of *cursus*: "Let the writer exert himself especially to adhere and keep to the Roman style, in other words at the conclusion of any utterance [*oracionis*] that makes complete sense [presumably any main clause] let there be a three-syllable expression followed by a four-syllable one." [38] In another treatise, the thirteenth-century *Summa* by Ludolf of Hildesheim, we find this curiously empty analogy: "as in a house there are three integral parts, foundation, wall, and roof, so in an epistle there are three integral parts, *exordium, narratio,* and *petitio,* and so the *salutatio* and *conclusio* of the true epistle do not seem essential." [39] The *Formularius de Modo Prosandi,* written at the beginning of the fourteenth century in the Cistercian Monastery of Baumgartenberg, is typical of the lot in its introductory part, wherein, except for one or two remarks on the salutation that make sense (though not all seem worth making), an outward appearance of system and precision conceals ideas that are variously jejune, vague, and mistaken.

Here begins the formulary "On how to write prose":

Know that for the attainment of clear and perspicuous form in the art of composing documents in prose according to the taste and usage of the present time, five points are to be especially noted to begin with concerning this same art: first what *dictare* means, second what *dictamen* means, third why those terms are used, fourth how the art originated, and fifth what and how many are its kinds.

Dictare means to explain the concepts of the mind in orderly fashion. *Dictamen* is therefore a worthy and artful congeries of words carrying a good freightage of thought, and nothing disjointed or superfluous. Thus the term *dictamen* is used to answer to the term *dictando,* in order that a given representation in writing may be suitable for the understanding of different persons, distinguished for the beauty of its words, and adorned with figures of thought. The origin or source of the art was two-fold: first in order that secrets might be kept between friends by means of *dictamen* or correspondence, wherefore we use the word *epistola,* from Greek "epistolon" which in Latin means "I conceal," second in order that the message may be better expressed. For a messenger entrusted with complicated business may not be able to remember all of it; for to be able to remember all things and have them at one's finger-tips is rather divine than human. There are three kinds of *dictamen: prosaicum, metricum,* and *rithmicum*; and one encounters also the *prosaicometricum,* which consists of both verse and prose, as the *dictamen* of Boethius does in certain passages. But we shall consider only prose *dictamen,* and pass by the others.

Know therefore that the terms *dictamen, epistola, kartha, littere,* as used in the present work are synonymous and stand for one and the same thing, and may be used interchangeably. An *epistola* is a message or memorandum [*libellus*] destined for an absent person or persons. The epistle arose out of certain particular causes as has been shown above. The parts of an epistle are five, to wit: *salutatio, exordium* or *benevolentie captatio, narratio, petitio,* and *conclusio.* At least two of these five parts must be included in every epistle: the *salutatio* and the *narratio,* or the *salutatio* and the *petitio.* First let us look at the *salutatio.*[40]

The rhetoric of drafting taught by Bentham in the nineteenth century and a not numerous but extremely able and influential company of lawyers writing in our time, some as members of official commissions, others as unofficial teachers or commentators, would appear to be the first that the world has seen in which the attempt has been made to offer instructions at once full and based on a thoughtful analysis of the purposes of this very special kind of writing. All of their work, so far as I know, has been devoted to the drafting of statutes or other official rules or regulations, but, as several of them notice, this hardly differs from the drafting of other instruments, unless it be a degree more exacting. I have been told that the best single treatment of the subject is the sixth chapter of Horace E. Read and John W. Macdonald's *Cases and Other Materials on Legislation.* The exposition of these writers is clear and readable, and they quote at length from a number of opinions, official reports, and monographs, a few dating back as much as a century or a little more, but most from the last two or three decades.

A few of the points on which the new school insists may be summarized as follows. Since laws are made by and for the citizen and only incidentally for judges and attorneys, they should be written in nonprofessional language.[41] The language should be accurate, but common. The ideals of accuracy and perspicuity seem to be set above all others. Thus one writer condemns the cultivation of "sonorous phrases or rhetorical flourishes";[42] and another speaks scornfully of draftsmen whose style betrays their anxiety "lest the words should fail to sound like the words of a legislature." [43] It is allowed, however, that "a statute on judicial procedure may properly use phrases that lawyers alone can comprehend, and even sentences as complex as those in legal treatises and law reviews." [44] Writers should all eschew the "tireless repetition" of reference words like "such," "aforesaid," and "hereinbefore." These, it is said, are superfluous, in view of the fact that people understand "stories, articles, and even legal treatises" written without them; and that apprehensions lest a "perverse judge will misinterpret the law by pretending to misunderstand it" are chimerical, since "we have to trust the judge anyway."[45] Sentences should be short.[46] A statute and each of its important divisions should be headed with a title.[47] Sections and subsections should be numbered.[48] Tabular form should be used for passages involving mathematics.[49] Single words should be used instead of phrases wherever possible.[50]

Laymen will be reassured to learn that lawyers believe it possible to iron out some, at least, of the difficulties that have beset the reading of instruments. Lawyers are the only experts who could make any headway with reform; and now that the profession has addressed itself to the problem, the lay critic may well hold his peace. But I will risk a further comment or two.

Bentham had already stated the ideal rule for the drafting of statutes: "make your meaning known and understood by every person of whom you expect he should act in consequence."[51] But there are a few other instruments besides statutes on judicial procedure in which technical terms would seem to be in order, notably wills, which not only often involve technical concepts, but are nearly always drawn, as they must always be probated, by legal specialists. Can Professor Rodell be serious in arguing that the technical terms of law ought to be abolished altogether?[52] Bentham, again, is surely right in allowing that "terms of art, jurisprudence must have as well as every other branch of art and science."[53]

Reference words can be overworked, but since readers of legal texts have motives for caviling that are unknown to typical readers of fiction or scientific exposition, it can hardly be proper to reason in this matter from the analogy of "stories, articles, and . . legal treatises." Nor must one forget the relation I have mentioned above between the traditional use of reference words and the rule, *still taught by the new authorities*, that the punctuation of an instrument is of no force. And by what logic can it be argued that because we have to trust the judge anyway, it makes no difference whether we adopt or reject a given mode of expression?

But the point on which I would most seriously question the new rhetoric is the sweeping rejection of language designed to suggest the solemnity of tradition. For the new idea is no mere rule of moderation: the statements I have cited about "sonorous phrases," "rhetorical flourishes," and the striving for an ancient-sounding style are categorical. Professor Rodell and two other critics, Jerome Frank and Stuart Chase, stand, like Read and Macdonald, for "realism," but take a far more radical point of view. These writers center their attack on words for broad concepts like "law," "equity," "justice," "prudence," "due care," "manifest intention," and so forth, which they consider mischievous on the ground that, although ostensibly clear, they are in fact vague. The radical reformers would purge legal writing of these and all terms suggestive of the idea of law as a dispensation to be deeply revered or of courts as competent to determine what constitutes "due care," "manifest intention," or the like, in any particular case.[54]

The position is plausible, but it surely involves two fallacies: first, that the terms of an instrument or the justice of a decision will be regarded with the same feelings by a party whom it stands to affect adversely as it will by the disinterested critic; and, second, that no two cases are alike.

The first fallacy is obvious from what I have spoken of as the coercive character of law. If men as a race were sufficiently intelligent and reasonable to respect law without thinking of it as having any force except that of reason, it should be possible for society to get rid of the "mystical" and most of the technical features of legal writing as well as the greater part of law itself. Disputes would seldom reach the courtroom; they would seldom arise. A simple literature of ethics could replace most of our statutes, and the most informal memoranda could serve in place of most or all formal instruments.

The second fallacy is of the perfectionist kind. It is true that no two cases are alike, for "circumstances alter cases." On the other hand, to abandon the conception of the case as a type would be to abandon all idea of law and precedent, and on a principle so fundamental that, if it were properly applicable to the abstractions of law, it would apply indifferently to all the abstractions that human thinking involves. Professor Rodell declares that legal principles have "no real or necessary relation to the solid substance of human affairs," [55] and Stuart Chase contrasts the "realities" of what "common folks . . . desperately need in the present" with "the trailing glories of the past." [56] Thurman Arnold is surely wiser. He includes the words "law," "equity," and "justice" among the "symbols of government" that he examines in his very interesting book by this name; and although he is quite as well aware as the radicals of the difficulties they present to lawyers, he recognizes that the problems of law involve morality as well as calculation and cannot be dealt with entirely in language of a high degree of precision. Noting that Soviet Russia, having attempted in 1917 to throw out legal theory in favor of practical convenience and establish a simple, commonsensical system of people's courts to supplant the entire existing judicial machinery, soon replaced these with a comparatively elaborate hierarchy of courts and founded schools of jurisprudence "dedicated to the development of a legal philosophy," Arnold goes on to remark that the resemblance of their present machinery and jurisprudence to ours is "startling," and "an interesting proof that the emotional cement which binds governments together, which gives them prestige and power, is not furnished by the realist, or by the scientist, but by priestly literature and ceremony." [57]

Professor John M. Maguire advises me that some of the best examples of drafting illustrative of the new theory are to be found in the work of an organization connected with the American Bar Association known as Commissioners on Uniform State Laws. This organization prepares and recommends for adoption statutes on various topics which can be handled in the same way throughout the country. Thus there is a uniform negotiable instruments law, a uniform sales act, and a number of other carefully drawn uniform statutes. He wrote me (under date of May 14, 1946) that

Some of the most skilful drafting of the last few years has been done by the American Law Institute, which has drawn not only some statutory proposals but also what are called "restatements," the latter being studious efforts to state American law with simplicity and brevity. The restatements are neither court decisions nor legislative enactments. They depend for their effect upon persuasive power and confidence in the ability of the authors.

Legislatures are, of course, much freer to make new departures in the style of their statutes than lawyers are in drawing private instruments, since they have the authority to repeal or amend enactments that experience proves faulty. Mere lawyers, having no similar power to rectify mistakes once made, are generally less inclined to use untested expressions. One of my lawyer friends, however, tells me that he has no fear concerning the reliability of plain language and uses it wherever possible in preference to standard jargon. He stands on the very interesting principle that court-tested jargon betrays its weakness by the very fact of its meaning ever having been open to dispute. But I believe that not many of his colleagues in the profession are so daring, their situation being well explained by the following part of a letter of June 4, 1946, that I owe to the kindness of Mr. Henry B. Hosmer of Boston:

In 1285 a statute was passed in England preventing the further extension of the subinfeudation of land. Of course, it became necessary to get around that statute as rapidly as possible and devious proceedings were invented to permit it. The language of these devious proceedings became the way of validly conveying land, and that language existed in deeds down to the beginning of the present century. It is still used by old-fashioned lawyers, particularly in the country, who draw their deeds by reference to form books in their offices which antedate their own practice. (It was necessary in order to dispense with the use of this meaningless language to pass statutes in most of the states which say that if A sells land to B, the deed reciting that A has sold land to B is enough.) This is merely ordinary caution on the part of lawyers. You can readily see that if someone comes into your office and is going to buy land for a good deal of money you want to be sure that the deed is a good deed. There are decisions in the books which say that if the deed contains certain language it is good, and so you don't take a chance and try to educate the legal profession to using modern English. You use the same old language, which you are sure of; and, until a statute comes to the rescue, that process continues indefinitely.

THE INDENTURE STYLE

To this understandable consideration, add that of the aesthetic appeal of the old lingo — no matter if reformers abhor it — and one may doubt that everyday drafting will ever be wholly modernized. The very injunctions of the new authorities against "rhetoric" indicate the force of the tradition behind it. Businesslike language expresses law in its practical aspect; "rhetoric," the instinct of which law itself is born.

INFLUENCES OF THE STYLE IN BELLES-LETTRES

The old-fashioned indenture style was a strong formative influence in various kinds of nonlegal English prose, particularly narrative prose, in the late Middle Ages and early Renaissance, diminishing gradually with men's increasing literary knowledge and consequent refinement of taste. The aristocratic, fastidious neoclassical mind very properly associated the *ars dictandi* with the "Gothic" past and the commercial, litigious, middle-class present, with the result that polite writers learned, in the course of the seventeenth century, to avoid it like the plague. The identity of the style in its more ostentatious manifestations was recognized, to be sure, as something distinct, special, and highflying already in the Middle Ages;[58] but it took long for men to become sensitive to its less obtrusive features. When at last almost all of its peculiar ways stood discredited for purposes of serious nonlegal, nonofficial expression, it thereby and thereupon became available to men of letters as a means to an occasional oblique effect.

The government of political units in the Middle Ages became increasingly systematic with the development of law and legal machinery by the rising legal profession, and the written word was an all-important means by which this development was carried forward. The official written word, moreover, in all its official solemnity was sure to reach every rank of society sooner or later, in one form or another — the upper ranks in a variety of documents and middle ranks in a lesser variety, but all ranks in publicly proclaimed decrees and other announcements made by royal heralds and town criers. At the same time we must not forget how limited was the circulation of the written word as the vehicle of unofficial literature before the in-

[115]

vention of printing. A wide variety of classical Latin poetry and belletristic prose had, of course, been preserved in the monasteries, and the manuscripts were being copied and recopied by cloistered scribes — mostly isolated from one another — along with the more voluminous, specifically Christian literature of Scripture, missals, hymns, sermons, and theological treatises; but the only nonlegalistic written literature that got widely communicated by word of mouth to the people at large was the prose and poetry of the Bible as translated or paraphrased from the Vulgate by the preachers.

Suppose, then, we imagine a churchman any time during the late Middle Ages sitting down to write a chronicle (and most of the chronicles were the work of churchmen), anxious to give his story a tone calculated to impress both ecclesiastical and lay readers with its elevated authority, and ask what models of style he would be likely to emulate. It would not be surprising if he decided to begin with a flourish of protocol and preamble after the manner of a royal or papal proclamation and then settled down in the body of his work to that most venerable of all narrative styles, a style familiar to all ears that had listened in church, Sunday after Sunday, to the biblical tales, whether read in Latin as part of the mass or offices or quoted in translation from the pulpit.

A medieval chronicle, as E. M. W. Tillyard has pointed out, typically recounted a central series of events illustrating a foreordained, divine plan, these events carrying the full weight of truth and significance without requiring to be analyzed, authenticated, or reasoned about; but the central theme was often surrounded with the byplay of a good deal of gossipy, miscellaneous story that the writer made no attempt to connect in any integral way with the main business.[59] For this kind of narrative, which simply states what happened with no ifs or buts — that Adam gave names to all cattle, that Semiramis built the city of Babylon, that Corineus slew the giant Gogmagog, and the like — the plain, paratactic style of the Bible was perfectly suited. If a chronicler taking this style for his model were to complicate it at all, he might be expected at most to lengthen his sentences with the trailing clauses introduced by "whereof," "wherefore," "whereby," and the like, beloved of the scriveners.

Our chronicler would know nothing of the Greek historians and probably not even Livy, but in any case the authority of the ancient pagans could not match that of Scripture, nor would their flexible, sophisticated prose have served as well as biblical prose as a model for the bare, chronicle kind of historiography. The Middle Ages produced a few writers capable of composing in the urbane, complex periods of classical prose — one could name William of Malmesbury, Geoffrey of Monmouth, and doubtless a fair number of other writers — but the medieval way of thinking was no stimulus to the cultivation of skill in this line, and it was only later that classical prose began to be widely imitated.

We find ideal examples of our hypothetical chronicler in several fifteenth-century translators of Latin and French chronicles discussed by Samuel K. Workman in his admirable study, *Fifteenth Century Translation as an Influence on English Prose*;[60] in writers of prose fiction of the same sort in Chaucer's ostensibly historical contemporary "Sir John Maundevile," whose *Voiage and Travaile*, translated from the French, was circulated in many manuscripts in the fifteenth century; and in sundry authors of popular chapbook tales of the sixteenth century. Our concern at the moment being only the influence of the *ars dictandi*, I will illustrate only this, referring the reader to Workman's book (particularly his second chapter) for samples of the paratactic, biblical prose of this period, or he may go directly to "Maundevile" or Malory's *Morte Darthur* or any of a number of anonymous texts that can be consulted conveniently in the publications of the Early English Text Society. In "Maundevile" it will be seen that the author tells his story in the "and . . . and . . . and . . ." way of the Old Testament, but opens his work with a sentence of the long-winded, legalistic kind, filling a page and a half of printed text. He gets lost in it, for there are constructions within it that do not fit the syntax of the enveloping period, but his intention is clear, because at the end he resumes and resolves the long-suspended thought with which he began.

Chaucer, as everybody knows, was a lively satirist of lawyers and their language, as when he remarks that the Man of Law "semed bisier than he was," when he makes the Host beg the Clerk to

Telle us som mery thing of aventures; —
Your termes, your colours, and your figures,
Kepe hem in stoor til so be ye endyte
Heigh style, as whan that men to kinges wryte,

or when, in the general Prologue, he thus characterizes the bibulous
Somnour:

And whan that he wel drunken hadde the wyn,
Than wolde he speke no word but Latyn.
A fewe termes hadde he, two or three,
That he had lerned out of som decree;
No wonder is, he herde it al the day;
And eek ye knowen wel, how that a Iay
Can clepen "Watte," as wel as can the pope.
But who-so coude in other thing him grope,
Thanne hadde he spent al his philosophye;
Ay "Questio quid iuris" wolde he crye.[61]

Yet Chaucer himself in his own prose *Tale of Melibeus* writes
very much like a scrivener, and with no apparent ironical intent,
for the same manner is evident in his *Treatise on the Astrolabe*. He
betrays the influence in his fondness for otiose doublets ("first and
forward," "of pitee and of mercy"), needless repetitions of workaday words, clauses beginning with "whereas" or more ponderous
conjunctions like "for-as-muche-as" and "al-be-it so that," trailing
result clauses introduced by "wherefore" and the like, demonstra-
tive and relative adjectives with names and other nouns ("this Melibeus," "this noble wyf Prudence," "the whiche three thinges"), and
stilted inversions of word order ("what ende that shal ther-of bifalle,
it is nat light to knowe").

Froissart's *Chronicles* as rendered by Lord Berners (1525), for
all the good passages they contain, nevertheless read at times like
an affidavit. The author constantly reminds us of his identity, uses
long compound and highly complex sentences bristling with the
usual whereases, wherefores, and doublets, relentlessly expands
dates and titles to maximum length, and at least once uses a nearly
exact equivalent of the legal formula "this writing witnesseth,"
namely, "Now sheweth the history that . . ." Well on in the book
we read:

Ye shall know that when I, sir John Froissart, author of this history, was departed from Orthez from the earl of Foix, as ye have heard herebefore, and went in company with the lord de la Rivière and the lord Guilliam of Tremouille, who brought the young duchess of Berry, daughter to the earl of Boulogne, to the duke of Berry, who wedded her in the town of Riom in Auvergne, as it is contained herebefore in this history; for at all these matters I was present, wherefore I may well speak thereof.[62]

He goes on with a description of an assembly of French lords and ladies in the vague and superlative language characteristic of legal preambles, so that the effect is nothing but a blur. A lady riding "a richly apparelled palfrey" loses her identity and interest when we find her in the company of another lady on "a palfrey richly apparelled," and the apparel of the two palfreys duplicated in richness, even verbatim, by that of the litters of sundry other ladies, even though they have different names.

The gradual sloughing off of the legalistic influence in historical writing between the chroniclers and the age of the Enlightenment can be observed clearly enough by anyone who will sample in order Berners's Froissart, Sir Thomas More's *History of Richard III*, Sir Walter Raleigh's *History of the World*, and Lord Clarendon's *History of the Rebellion*. It is the outward sign of a profound twofold change in men's conception of the nature of history. Not only did the medieval idea of history as divinely predetermined give way to that of history as a series of events whose relations and meaning need to be discovered and explained by an effort of the reason, but also truthfulness came to be seen as an intellectual and not merely a moral virtue and therefore a quality to be made manifest by documentation, whereas the old-fashioned writer assumed he could carry conviction by writing in a style suggestive of Scripture and/or of the good faith of a party to a legal transaction acting under oath, perhaps explicitly protesting his veracity, like a deponent.

Satire of lawyers and their lingo in Rabelais, Nashe, Shakespeare, Beaumont and Fletcher, and dozens of other Renaissance writers runs considerably ahead of any general liberation of prose composition from the legalistic incubus. These writers cannot be unashamedly and consciously affecting the thing they hold up to ridicule, yet it is easy to spot sooner or later in the prose of nearly all of them the scrivener's mannerisms, for these had become virtually a part of the idiom — not just of the English language but, I believe, of all the contemporary languages of Europe. In Elizabethan prose the most pervasive legacy of the scrivener is the long, meandering sentence, with its wherefores, wherebys, and the like; but we also notice a fairly general fondness for doublets, vague superlatives, and a parade of full-length honorific titles and dates.

It remains to notice an illustration or two of the occasional oblique effects that sophisticated writers have known how to insinuate by dropping momentarily into the draftsman's manner.

The least subtle of these are attempts to put legalistic pedantry in a comic light by the clumsy expedient of a full-dress display of it in complete documents, like the challenge sent by the jester Wamba to Front de Boeuf in *Ivanhoe*, or the constitution of the Pickwick Club. Such passages are only one amongst other expressions of the overfed complacency that inflated so much nineteenth-century prose, as it did Victorian furniture, tradesmen's bellies, and female bosoms. A happy contrast can be cited from the eighteenth century in *Tristram Shandy* (1760–67), for Sterne knew how to turn the trick. He filled a whole chapter (III, xi) with the formal curse supplied by "my father" and applied, at his insistence, by Dr. Slop to the latter's servant Obadiah for the tight knots this fellow has tied in the doctor's bag; but it goes like a breeze, thanks to its absurd wealth of concrete detail, Uncle Toby's whistled accompaniment to the reading of it, and the interjections of the listeners ("Our armies swore terribly in Flanders, cried my Uncle Toby, — but nothing to this!").

The subtler effects, if I am not mistaken, are all of one general kind, differing only in the degree of their pungency. A writer may identify a person in high place with a slightly more ceremonious title than necessary, not quite to satirize him, but simply to recall the greater degree of reverence with which all potentates were once regarded than any is today; or he may intend satire, more or less mordant.

In his sympathetic history of the Spanish Armada from the Spanish point of view Garrett Mattingly makes use of ceremonious language to cast a pall of somber foreboding over the parting visit paid by the admiral (known as the Captain General) — the great and good Duke of Medina Sidonia — and other personnel of the expedition to the Cathedral of Lisbon to receive the Church's benediction. The writer has dwelt on the Duke's profound original reluctance to accept the leadership of the enterprise and his awareness now that his preparations were far from adequate. So the ceremony in the cathedral, at least to us who know the upshot of the voyage, is — but also was, in all probability, to the unhappy admiral as well — ominous, and the more so to us for the slight hints of official formality in the style in which the historian describes it:

Now the Captain General went solemnly to the cathedral, accompanied by His Most Catholic Majesty's Viceroy, the Cardinal Archduke. The Archbishop of Lisbon, himself, said mass and pronounced a general benediction on the Enterprise. The standard was lifted from the altar and borne across the Plaza Mayor to the Dominican convent where the duke himself laid it on that altar in token of his personal dedication. Then the banner was borne back between kneeling lines of soldiers and sailors to whom friars read the papal absolution and indulgence granted to all partakers in this most holy crusade. On the blessed banner, on one side of the arms of Spain was the image of Christ crucified, on the other of His Holy Mother. Beneath was a scroll with the words of the psalmist, *"Exurge, domine, et vindica causam tuam"* — Arise, O Lord, and vindicate thy cause.[63]

On the other hand, the effect may be, as not seldom in Gibbon, devastating irony. Such is the sting of this writer's bland reference to the papal pretender of the fifteenth century who called himself John XXIII by an epithet ("the vicar of Christ") traditionally belonging to the papal incumbent: "the most scandalous charges were suppressed; the vicar of Christ was only accused of piracy, murder, rape, sodomy, and incest"; and in the same vein, of the eleventh-century Pope John XII: "his rapes of virgins and widows had deterred the female pilgrims from visiting the tomb of St. Peter, lest, in the devout act, they should be violated by his successor."[64]

In prose fiction, no genre has been more of a favorite than the biographical or autobiographical novel, and many a writer in this genre has shown himself aware that his hero is of small account, as to either status or accomplishment, by comparison with the great men celebrated in the ultimate models of this new, bourgeois form — the old epics, romances, chronicles, saints' lives, and classical histories. Who is Jack Wilton or Tom Jones or Pamela Andrews beside Achilles or Dido, Sir Lancelot or Isolde, St. George or Richard of the lion heart? And how better might a novelist acknowledge the incongruity of his composing a quasi-epic about such a nobody than by introducing this person with a mildly ironical flourish of protocol and preamble?

In the long, suspended sentence that opens Nashe's novel, the picaresque Jack Wilton is made to introduce himself as if making a deposition, and clearly betrays his awareness of being a comparative nobody by the care he takes to protest that he is "a gentleman at least."

The "I, John Doe" formula opens several novels of the eighteenth and nineteenth centuries, with various nuances of connotation, and the genealogical opening in the third person is also a favorite. The fellow represented as the reporter of Smollett's *The Adventures of an Atom* (1769) is "I, Nathaniel Peacock, of the parish of St. Giles's, haberdasher and author," and he proceeds in the same legalistic fashion as Nashe's Jack Wilton: "[I] . . . solemnly declare that, on the third of last August, sitting alone in my study, up three pair of stairs, between the hours of eleven and twelve at night, meditating [notice the ponderous diction] upon the uncertainty of sublunary enjoyment, I heard a shrill, small voice," etc., etc. Subtlety is no object with either Nashe or Smollett, and we may choose, according to taste, between the ways in which they leaven the wordy prose of the spokesmen of these novels: pervasive, gay impudence in Jack Wilton's manner of recalling episodes of mischief and horror, and the poker-faced sobriety of Nathaniel Peacock as he goes on to retail indecencies more bald and gross than the most extreme to be found in Rabelais.

These pieces, of course, are far from typical novels, and their art is all but transparent compared to the soberer art of standard nineteenth-century fiction, the chief characters of which are neither heroes nor knaves or fools but rather people of average, decent instincts and middling caliber, like our own relatives and friends. If a novelist introduces a central character of this kind in language that hints, ever so slightly, at the style of a formal memorial, the result is a double effect. A family tree is a dignity, but grows, like a real tree, only by a process of accretion, not by stretching, and therefore fixes the place of the individual immovably in relation to both forebears and posterity. Hence, while it dignifies all the names on its roots and branches, it is also, of each, something like an epitaph or epitaph-to-be. So it is no wonder that in Thackeray's *Henry Esmond* (1852) we sense in the initial paragraph of the first chapter, concerned as it is with genealogy and family portraits, the faintly somber atmosphere of nostalgia that hangs over the whole story. We read that "Francis, fourth Viscount Castlewood, came to his title, and presently after to take possession of his house of Castlewood, county Hants, in the year 1691." If Francis was the fourth Viscount, then earlier ones had ceased to be, and the phrase "the year 1691" has just a hint more of formality than the mere number would have, as if to say *"requiescat"* to this Francis, his cousin Henry, and the whole of the two generations they represented.

One would not perhaps call the faint implications of the passage irony; but a mild irony does seem clearly intended in the opening sentence of Maria Edgeworth's *Castle Rackrent* (1800), which is likewise devoted to genealogy: "Sir Condy Rackrent, by the grace of God heir-at-law to the Castle Rackrent, was a remote branch of the family."

A convenient example of the legalistic "I, John Doe" formula used to good effect to support the portrayal of the persona as an unliterary, homespun character is offered by the opening of R. D. Blackmore's now despised novel, *Lorna Doone* (1869); and the same expedient with much the same purpose had been used by John Galt for both the beginning and ending of the introductory chapter of *Annals of the Parish* (1821), with the difference that the persona here, though vastly naïve, is not without book learning. In fact the Reverend Micah Balwhidder once thought of writing "an orthodox poem, like *Paradise Lost*, by John Milton,"[65] and would have written his wife's epitaph in Latin but for the fact that she, "worthy woman as she was, did not understand the Latin tongue . . . nor" — he discovered — "would it have been easy, as I found upon experimenting, to tell what I had to tell in Latin, which is naturally a crabbed language, and very difficult to write properly."[66] The kind of formality he likes to affect — and it is conspicuous throughout the story — is therefore no *pis aller* of ignorance but the free choice of a tolerably well-instructed, if very quaint and limited, mind. Here are the relevant passages:

In the same year, and on the same day of the same month, that his Sacred Majesty King George, the third of the name, came to his crown and kingdom, I was placed and settled as the minister of Dalmailing. When about a week thereafter this was known in the parish, it was thought a wonderful thing, and everybody spoke of me and the new king as united in our trusts and temporalities, marvelling how the same should come to pass, and thinking the hand of Providence was in it, and that surely we were pre-ordained to fade and flourish in fellowship together; which has really been the case: for in the same season that his Most Excellent Majesty, as he was very properly styled in the proclamations for the general fasts and thanksgivings, was set by as a precious vessel which had received a crack or a flaw, and could be serviceable in the way of an ornament, I was obliged, by reason of age and the growing infirmities of my recollection, to consent to the earnest entreaties of the Session, and to accept of Mr. Amos to be my helper.

Then Mr. Dalziel, who was always a composed and sedate man, said a few words of prayer, and I was comforted therewith, and rose to go home to the manse; but in the churchyard all the congregation was assembled, young and old, and they made a lane for me to the back-yett that opened into the manse-garden — Some of them put out their hands and touched me as I passed, followed by the elders, and some of them wept. It was as if I was passing away, and to be no more — verily, it was the reward of my ministry — a faithful account of which, year by year, I now set down, in the evening of my days, to make up, to the end that I may bear witness to the work of a beneficent Providence, even in the narrow sphere of my parish, and the concerns of that flock of which it was His most gracious pleasure to make me the unworthy shepherd.[67]

Notes

NOTES

Introductory Remarks

THE TERMS "PROSE" AND "STYLE" EXAMINED

1 In classical Latin the noun "versus" signified simply a line of writing, whether metrical (as in Cicero's *De Oratore*, II, 257) or nonmetrical (as in the same work at I, 261). Quintilian uses the word both ways (in *Institutiones Oratoriae*: for the nonmetrical line at X, i, 38; for the metrical, at I, v, 18); but he also uses the expressions not found in Cicero, "prosa oratio" (I, v, 18) and "prosa" (I, viii, 2), to refer to nonmetrical discourse when he wishes explicitly to contrast this with verse. "Prosa" is, of course, simply short for "prorsa," which in turn is short for "proversa" or "provorsa" ("vorto" being an oft-recorded variant of "verto").

2 Comment on Terence's *Eunuchus*, II, iii, 14; cited by Ethan Allen Andrews, *Latin-English Lexicon* (New York: Harper, 1869), voc. *prorsus* 2.II.

3 Nor has R. W. Chambers in his justly famous essay, "On the Continuity of English Prose from Alfred to More and His School" (London: Humphrey Milford, Oxford University Press, 1932, published for the Early English Text Society). Chambers proves and illustrates the continuity of a literature, not of a style. His concern is to exhibit the early development of the resources of our vernacular to meet divers requirements and to show that the history of English prose, though not of any one genre, is unbroken from its beginnings. He finds that at the accession of Henry II "English historical prose . . . after a life of some ninety years following the Conquest" disappears for three centuries, but that during these centuries there flourished a fine literature of sermons and devotional manuals (pp. lxxxviii–xc).

4 See my account of Alberic of Monte Cassino and other writers on the *ars dictandi* in the sixth chapter below, pp. 107–110.

5 R. R. Bolgar, *The Classical Heritage and Its Beneficiaries* (Cambridge: Cambridge University Press, 1954), Ch. I, "The Background," especially Part i, "The Character of the Classical Heritage," pp. 13–26.

6 C. S. Baldwin, *Medieval Rhetoric and Poetic* (New York: Macmillan, 1928), p. 10.

7 *De Oratore*, III, 59.

8 *Orator*, §§37–42.

9 *Rhetorica ad Herennium*, IV, 28–32.

10 Baldwin, *Medieval Rhetoric and Poetic*, p. 43.

11 *Ibid.*, p. 5.

12 *De Oratore*, II, 62, 64, 65.

13 *Ibid.*, II, 70.

14 *The Works of Thomas Gray*, ed. by Edmund Gosse (4 vols.; New York: Stokes, 1895), Vol. II, pp. 109, 110, cited by Jeremiah Wesley Bray, *A History of English Critical Terms* (Boston: Heath, 1898), p. 166.

15 "The Study of Poetry," *Essays in Criticism*, 2nd Series (London: Macmillan, 1888), p. 39, cited by Bray, *History of English Critical Terms*, p. 45.

16 Let us note in passing that R. W. Chambers, in demonstrating "the continuity of English prose from Alfred to More," makes it no part of his thesis to deny that this prose was developed under nonnative influences. All of it, needless to say — chronicles, sermons, and devotional manuals — was written in emulation of Latin antecedents, and with such enterprise, by and large, that what turns out to be exceptional in the West Saxon of the pre-Conquest period is not its capacity to articulate learned discourse: the exceptional phenomenon is the distinctly native, non-Latin, "tumbling" style of certain of Aelfric's homilies, particularly the one on St. Cuthbert (from which an extract is quoted below, p. 59), a style positively primitive by comparison with what we find in both earlier and later West Saxon pieces, including some of Aelfric's own. A. J. Wyatt remarks of the St. Cuthbert sermon that "it is marred by excessive alliteration, indicating in all probability that it was originally delivered with a loose, sing-song rhythm." A. J. Wyatt, ed., *An Anglo-Saxon Reader* (Cambridge: Cambridge University Press, 1919), p. 234.

17 *De Oratore*, II, 62.

18 *Orator*, XIX, 65, cf. 37.

19 Quintilian, X, i, 31.

The Deliberative Style

THE STYLE OF PERSUASION

1 Here is a full tally of the parts of the full-dress deliberative oration defined by one or more of the Roman authorities. These authorities agree both as to the main sections to be distinguished in most good speeches and their order, and also as to the propriety of varying the pattern more or less to meet particular needs: (1) introductory remarks (the "exordium"); (2) statement of the background of the case or issue (the "narratio"); (3) statement of the thesis (the "propositio"); (4) announcement of the headings under which the thesis is to be argued (the "distributio"); (5) the argument proper (the "confirmatio"); (6) refutation of opposing arguments that have been or may be expected to be heard (the "reprehensio" or "refutatio"); (7) an excursus on some matter tangent to the thesis (the "digressio"); and (8) the conclusion (or "peroratio"). See the anonymous *Rhetorica ad Herennium* (B.C. 86–82[?]), III, 4; Cicero, *De Oratore*, I, 143; and Quintilian, III, ix, and IV.

2 See, for example, Cicero's *De Oratore*, II, 307–314; Quintilian, V, xii, 14.

3 Cicero, *De Oratore*, I, 144; III, 38ff; Quintilian, III, ii, 36, viii, 62–65; VIII, i and ii.

4 Cicero, *De Oratore*, III, 124, 125; *Brutus* § 50; *Orator* § 97; Quintilian, IV, ii, 44.

NOTES

5 Quintilian concedes that for a speaker "to express confidence in himself is sometimes allowable"; and he finds most of Cicero's boasting legitimate, citing that great orator's need to resort to it by way of defense of himself and his aids in suppressing the Catilinian conspiracy (XI, i, 1–25). He nowhere states the principle I have here put forward, but comes near it in a negative way when he remarks that "though every kind of self-laudation is unbecoming" (15), self-confidence in a speaker "is sometimes justified by his age, dignity, or authority" (28). Much weight, it seems to me, should be attached to the example of unashamed self-praise so often given by Cicero, whether or not it be judged excessive. In Burke's speech "On Conciliation with America," the whole exordium, which fills over four and a half printed octavo pages, is mainly about Edmund Burke, and the first personal pronoun is conspicuous in over half of the sentences.

6 Thus Gilbert Highet, *The Classical Tradition* (New York and London: Oxford University Press, 1949), p. 323.

7 Quintilian, IX, iv, 31.

8 Fourth Oration against Catiline.

9 Plato, *Gorgias, passim*; Aristotle, *Rhetoric*, III, i, 5 (1404a). Socrates, of course, expounds an ideal rhetoric in the *Phaedrus*; and Aristotle's reason for expounding the art is "not its being right, but necessary" (*loc. cit.*: οὐκ ὀρθῶς ἔχοντος, ἀλλ' ὡς ἀναγκαίου).

10 Francis Bacon, *The Advancement of Learning* (1605) (London: Oxford University Press, 1906), I, iv, 2; on the Royal Society's stand against "all amplification, digressions, and swellings of style" and for "a close, naked, natural way of speaking, positive expressions, clear senses, a native easiness, bringing all things as near the mathematical plainness as they can," see Thomas Sprat's *History of the Royal Society of London* (1667), from whom these oft-quoted expressions are taken (cited from *The Cambridge History of English Literature* (14 vols.; New York: Putnam, 1907–17), Vol. VIII, p. 422), and the full and careful treatment given the subject by George Williamson in *The Senecan Amble* (Chicago: University of Chicago Press, 1951), Ch. 9. To jump to the twentieth century, Robert Graves and Alan Hodge declare, in *The Reader Over Your Shoulder* (New York: Macmillan, 1943), p. 37, that "an English writer with something to say needs no rhetorical art."

11 By Rudolf Flesch (New York and London: Harper, 1946).

12 *Iliad*, II, 337–374, trans. by Andrew Lang, Walter Leaf, and Ernest Myers (New York: Modern Library, 1929), pp. 28–30.

13 M. O. Hazeltine, ed., *Orations from Homer to McKinley* (25 vols.; New York: Collier, 1902), Vol. V, p. 2117.

14 *Ibid.*, p. 2119.

15 *Ibid.*, pp. 2137, 2145.

16 *Ibid.*, pp. 2120, 2122, 2128, 2133, 2140.

17 *Ibid.*, pp. 2130, 2136, 2138.

18 *Ibid.*, pp. 2127–2128.

19 John Chipman Gray recognizes that a court may have "not to determine what the legislature did mean on a point which was present to its mind [in the making of a given statute], but to guess what it would have intended on a point not present to its mind, if the point had been present" in *The Nature and Sources of the Law* (New York: Columbia University Press, 1909), p. 370, quoted by Roscoe Pound and T. F. T. Plucknett, *Readings*

on the History and System of the Common Law, 3rd ed. (Rochester, N.Y.: Lawyers Co-operative, 1927), p. 42.

20 Erasmus, *Ciceronianus*, trans. by Izora Scott (New York: Teachers College, Columbia University, 1908), pp. 113–114.

21 *The Advancement of Learning*, I, iv, 2, pp. 27, 28.

22 Folios liv ⱽ–lix ʳ.

23 Erasmus, *Ciceronianus*, pp. 113–114.

24 *Opera Omnia*, ed. by David Ruhnken (4 vols. in 2; Leyden, 1789), Oration xxii, delivered in Rome in January 1572, new style, Vol. I, pp. 173–179.

25 Hazeltine, *Orations from Homer to McKinley*, Vol. II, pp. 440–443. The translator is not named.

26 *The History of the Peloponnesian War*, trans. by Richard Crawley (New York: Dutton (Everyman's Library), 1910), pp. 606–607.

27 *Middlemarch* (New York, 1884), pp. 626–627.

The Expository Style

TREATISE · LESSON · SERMON

1 Stuart Chase makes the interesting remark that "Over the movie we tend to feel emotion, over the stills, to think." *The Tyranny of Words* (New York: Harcourt, Brace, 1938), p. 44.

2 Aristotle, *Organon*, I, v, trans. and ed. by O. F. Owen (2 vols.; London: Bohn, 1889), Vol. I, p. 91.

3 From H. W. T. Wager, "Plants: Cytology," *Encyclopaedia Britannica*, 13th ed., XXI, 769; here quoted with the kind permission of Encyclopaedia Britannica.

4 From Charles Darwin, *The Origin of Species*, Ch. IV, quoted here from W. S. Knickerbocker, ed., *Classics of Modern Science* (New York: Crofts, 1936), pp. 226–227.

5 *Ibid.*, 234.

6 *Ibid.*, 230.

7 *Ibid.*, 241.

8 See John Lyly, *Euphues*, ed. by M. W. Croll and Harry Clemens (London: Routledge; New York: Dutton, 1916), Introduction, especially pp. xxxix–xlvi, lx–lxiv.

9 XII, x, 58. Quintilian expressly cites the Greek terms.

10 According to G. L. Hendrickson, "The earliest occurrence of the threefold division is in the *Auctor ad Herennium*" (IV, viii, 11). "The Origin and Meaning of the Ancient Characters of Style," *American Journal of Philology*, Vol. XXVI (1905), p. 268. The *Ad Herennium* is of unknown authorship and of date between B.C. 88 and 82, according to Harry Caplan, editor and translator of the text in the Loeb Classical Library edition (Cambridge, Mass.: Harvard University Press, 1954), pp. xiv, xxvi.

11 Cicero, *Orator*, XIX, 65; XX, 69; XXVI, 96; Quintilian, XII, x, 58, 59.

12 *Orator*, XI, 37–XII, 39; XIII, 42.

13 *Ibid.*, XIX, 62.

14 *Ibid.*, 63.

15 *Ibid.*, 65.

16 *Ibid.*, XX, 69.

17 *Ibid.*, XXVI, 91.

NOTES

18 *Ibid.*, XXVII, 95.

19 ". . . even the style of their discourse, though possibly subtle and undoubtedly penetrating, yet for an orator is bald, unfamiliar, jarring on the ear of the public, devoid of clarity ["obscurum"], [and devoid of] fulness ["ieiunum"]." Cicero, *De Oratore*, III, xviii, 66. "Stoic oratory is too closely knit and too compact for a popular audience." Cicero, *Brutus*, XXXI, 120.

20 Robert Scott and W. C. Stiles, eds., *Modern Sermons by World Scholars* (10 vols.; New York and London: Funk & Wagnalls, 1909), Vol. V, p. 3.

21 *Ibid.*, p. 5.

22 *Ibid.*, pp. 14, 15.

23 Quoted from A. J. Wyatt, ed., *An Anglo-Saxon Reader* (Cambridge: Cambridge University Press, 1919), pp. 73–75.

24 John Lyly, *Euphues and His England*, 1580, ed. by Edward Arber (London: Constable, 1919), p. 297.

25 *Euphues: The Anatomy of Wit*, 1579, ed. by Edward Arber (London: Constable, 1919), p. 45.

26 *The Collected Works of Abraham Lincoln*, ed. by Roy P. Basler, 9 vols. (New Brunswick, N.J.: Rutgers University Press, 1953), Vol. III, p. 23. Of the five known texts in Lincoln's hand, this is the latest, written some time after March 4, 1864. *Ibid.*, p. 22, n. 33.

The Tumbling Style

ITS ORIGIN AND INCIDENCE

Epigraph: Chaucer's Host in the prologue to *The Tale of Melibeus*, line 7, commenting on the poet's *Tale of Sir Thopas*. I take it that the Host is drawing a comparison and not making a literal statement, meaning to express a generally derogatory opinion of *The Tale of Sir Thopas*; but either way the derogatory sense of the word "dogerel" must be supposed to derive mainly from verse of the native tradition (whether or not ornamented with the single new feature of rhyme), as opposed to verse of the wholly new kind that Chaucer was writing. In the sixteenth century both of the terms "dogerel" and "tumbling verse" were current and both were defined by early writers as referring to any sort of irregular verse (see the *New English Dictionary*); but since in nearly all the verse of that century that was irregular by the standards of the new system introduced by Wyatt and Surrey (or reintroduced, now that Chaucer's use of it had been lost to view), we can recognize the backbone of the old native line, namely four dominant stresses standing out among a loose assortment of from three to a dozen or more unstressed or half-stressed syllables, either term may properly be used to refer primarily — any time since *Piers Plowman* — not to the whole indeterminate category of bad, trivial, or irregular verse, but to verse showing positive features that place it in a recognizable tradition unbroken from Anglo-Saxon times to the early years of the seventeenth century.

1 *Beowulf*, 736–745, my translation.

2 William Langland, *Piers the Plowman*, B-text, Passus V, 188–199, quoted from the edition of W. W. Skeat, 9th ed. (Oxford: Clarendon, 1906), pp. 49–50.

3 *The Homilies of the Anglo-Saxon Church*, ed. by Benjamin Thorpe (2 vols.; London: Aelfric Society, 1844–46), Vol. II, No. 10; my translation.

PROSE STYLES

4 *The Rise of English Literary Prose* (New York: Oxford University Press, 1915), p. 55.

5 *Ibid.*, pp. 61, 62. These tracts can be regarded as the missing link in the evolution of Elizabethan pamphleteering prose out of the old poetry. The prose was not merely influenced by the poetry, but was its direct offspring. Of *Jacke Upland, The Reply of Friar Daw Topias*, and *Jacke Upland's Rejoinder*, J. P. Oakden remarks that "The metre of these poems is so corrupt and crude that the usual investigation is quite impossible. Thus in *Jacke Upland* about one-sixth of the lines have two alliterating syllables, whereas the rest have no alliteration . . . The metre of *The Reply* and of *The Rejoinder* is not quite so formless, alliteration being found in a third of the lines of the former poem, and in a quarter of those of the latter poem. Some accurate half-lines can be found . . . Beneath the formlessness can be observed the older system, but the decay is complete." Oakden, *Alliterative Poetry in Middle English: Dialectal and Metrical Survey* (Manchester: Manchester University Press, 1930–35), pp. 180, 181.

6 Krapp, *The Rise of English Literary Prose*, pp. 83–90.

7 *Ibid.*, p. 128.

8 *The Works of Thomas Nashe*, ed. by Ronald B. McKerrow (5 vols.; London: Sidgwick & Jackson, 1910), Vol. III, pp. 198–199. I have here emended the beginning of the second sentence, which in McKerrow's 1910 edition reads "The gods, and gods and goddesses."

9 Bernard DeVoto, *We Accept with Pleasure* (Boston: Little, Brown, 1934), pp. 16, 17; here quoted with kind permission of the author.

10 *Pantagruel*, Book IV, Ch. 19.

11 Jonathan Swift, "A Voyage to the Country of the Houyhnhnms," *Gulliver's Travels*, 1726 (London: Humphrey Milford; Oxford University Press, 1902, 1924), Part iv, Ch. 6, p. 237.

12 In *Select Works of Tobias Smollett*, with Prefatory Memoir by Sir Walter Scott (2 vols.; New York: Stringer & Townsend, n.d.), Vol. II, p. 478.

13 Laurence Sterne, *Tristram Shandy*, Book VIII, Ch. 3.

14 Paul Stapfer, *Laurence Sterne — Sa Personne et Ses Ouvrages* (Paris: E. Thorin, 1870), p. 143.

15 Joel Chandler Harris, *Nights with Uncle Remus* (Boston: Osgood, 1883, reprinted 1911), p. 123.

The Prophetic Style

BIBLICAL PROPHECY · STOIC PHILOSOPHY · THE ESSAY

1 J. A. K. Thomson, *The Classical Background of English Literature* (London: Allen & Unwin, 1948), pp. 20, 24.

2 E. Vernon Arnold, *Roman Stoicism* (Cambridge: Cambridge University Press, 1911), pp. 414–435.

3 M. W. Croll, "Attic Prose in the Seventeenth Century," *Studies in Philology*, Vol. XVIII (1921), p. 111.

4 See M. W. Croll, "The Baroque Style in Prose, 1575–1675" in *Studies in English Philology: A Miscellany in Honor of Frederick Klaeber*, ed. by Kemp Malone and M. B. Ruud (Minneapolis: University of Minnesota Press, 1929), especially p. 430. Bacon advises that "knowledge that is delivered as a thread to be spun on ought to be delivered and intimated, if it were possible, in the same method wherein it was invented . . . if you will have sciences

NOTES

grow, it is less matter for the shaft or body of the tree, so you look well to the taking up of the roots." *The Advancement of Learning*, II, xvii, 4, pp. 150–151.

5 Diogenes Laertius, *Lives of Eminent Philosophers*, VII, 59, ed. and trans. by R. D. Hicks (2 vols.; London: Heinemann; New York: Putnam (Loeb Classical Library), 1925), Vol. II, pp. 167–168.

6 Croll, "Attic Prose in the Seventeenth Century," pp. 114–116; Hendrickson, "The Origin and Meaning of the Ancient Characters of Style," *American Journal of Philology*, Vol. XXVI (1905), pp. 258–259. The relevant *locus* in Aristotle is *Rhetoric*, III, vii, 4–5, and *loci* in Cicero, *Orator*, XXI, 71, and XXXV, 123.

7 Diogenes Laertius, *Lives of Eminent Philosophers*, VII, 18, in Vol. II, p. 129.

8 *Ibid.*, VII, 187–188, in Vol. II, p. 297.

9 *Brutus*, XXXI, 117, 120; *De Oratore*, III, xviii, 66.

10 From Epictetus's *Discourses*, IV, x, in *The Works of Epictetus*, trans. by Thomas Wentworth Higginson, new and revised ed. (2 vols.; Boston: Little, Brown, 1890), Vol. II, pp. 194–195.

11 Seneca, *Moral Essays*, with an English trans. by John W. Basore (3 vols.; London: Heinemann; New York: Putnam (Loeb Classical Library), 1928), Vol. I, p. x.

12 Nor has his moral character escaped criticism. See Moses Hadas, *A History of Latin Literature* (New York: Columbia University Press, 1952), pp. 245–246.

13 X, i, 129, 130.

14 *Suetonius, The Lives of the Caesars*, with an English trans. by J. C. Rolfe (2 vols.; London: Heinemann; New York: Macmillan (Loeb Classical Library), 1914), Book IV (Gaius Caligula), LIII, 2, in Vol. I, p. 485.

15 *Characteristics of Men, Manners, Opinions, Times, etc.* (1711), ed. by John M. Robertson (London: G. Richards, 1900), cited from George Williamson, *The Senecan Amble* (Chicago: University of Chicago Press, 1951), p. 353.

16 *De Ira*, II, xxxii, my translation.

17 *Essays by Francis Bacon* (1625), ed. by Geoffrey Grigson (London: Oxford University Press, 1902, 1940), pp. 5–6.

18 *The Works of Sir Thomas Browne*, ed. by Simon Wilkin (3 vols.; London: Bohn, 1899), Vol. II, pp. 562–563.

19 From "Crabbed Age and Youth," *The Works of Robert Louis Stevenson* (22 vols.; New York: Scribner, 1900), Vol. XIII, p. 61.

20 "Mental Vice," *Trivia* (Garden City, N.Y.: Doubleday, Page, 1921), p. 96, here quoted with the kind permission of Doubleday and Company, Inc.

21 *Ibid.*

22 *How to Live on Twenty-Four Hours a Day* (New York: Doran, 1910), pp. 16–17, here quoted with the kind permission of Doubleday and Company, Inc.

23 "Virginibus Puerisque," *Works*, Vol. XIII, pp. 5–6.

24 "A Dissertation upon Roast Pig," *The Essays of Elia*, ed. by Alfred Ainger (New York: International Book, 1890), p. 169.

25 "Too Many Books," *Selected Modern Essays* (London: Oxford University Press, 1925), p. 362.

26 For evidence see M. W. Croll, "Muret and the History of Attic Prose,"

PROSE STYLES

Publications of the Modern Language Association, Vol. XXXIX (1924), pp. 267–268. Croll here quotes a remarkable passage from the Jesuit teacher Comenius, and mentions that Roger Ascham held a similar view. In Ascham's *The Scholemaster* (1570) we find Aristotle and Cicero treated as gods of Anglican, as in Comenius's view they are gods of Catholic, orthodoxy: "For he that can neither like Aristotle in Logicke and Philosophie, nor Tullie in Rhetoricke and Eloquence, will, from these steppes, likelie enough presume, by like pride to mount higher, to the misliking of greater matters: that is either in Religion to have a dissentious head, or in the common wealth, to have a factious heart . . ." Ed. by Edward Arber (London: Constable, 1925), p. 93.

27 From Chapter I, "Phenomena," of Book III, "The Modern Worker," of Thomas Carlyle's *Past and Present* (1843) (London: Oxford University Press, 1909), pp. 143–144.

28 Rev. ed. (New York: Scribner, 1922), Ch. XV, pp. 143–144.

29 Thornton Wilder's preface to Gertrude Stein, *The Geographical History of America or the Relation of Human Nature to the Human Mind* (New York: Random House, 1936), p. 14.

30 From *The Childermass* (London: Chatto and Windus, 1928), p. 92, here quoted with the kind permission of Mrs. Wyndham Lewis and the present holder of the copyright, Methuen & Co. Ltd.

31 From James Joyce, *Finnegans Wake* (London: Faber and Faber, 1939), p. 253; quoted with the kind permission of Faber and Faber Ltd.

The Indenture Style

LEGAL DOCUMENTS · PRIVATE FORMAL MESSAGES

Epigraph: "It is said in an old case in regard to candle-making in a town, 'Le utility del chose excusera le noisomeness del stink . . .' " Sir James Fitzjames Stephen, *A General View of the Criminal Law of England* (London and New York: Macmillan, 1890), p. 106. I owe this reference to my friend William Prosser, sometime professor of law in the University of Minnesota.

1 *Uncle Remus, His Songs and His Sayings* (New York: Appleton, 1911), p. 21.

2 Howard Willis Preston, *Documents Illustrative of American History 1606–1863* (New York: Putnam, 1886), p. 56.

3 *Ibid.*, pp. 44, 45.

4 John Bouvier, *Law Dictionary*, new ed. by Francis Rawle (2 vols.; Boston: Boston Book, 1897), under "punctuation." These conventions have not changed perceptibly, if at all. E. E. Brossard repeats that "Punctuation is no part of the statute," and states that "The law of England is the same as ours" in this regard. "Punctuation of Statutes," *Report of the Committee on Legislative Drafting, National Conference of Commissioners on Uniform State Laws*, 1938, quoted by Horace E. Read and John W. MacDonald, *Cases and Other Materials on Legislation* (Brooklyn: Foundation Press, 1948), p. 951.

5 Horace E. Read, *Regulations Revision Committee Manual, Canadian Naval Service*, 1943, § V, 1, vii, ix, quoted in Read and MacDonald, *Cases*, p. 960.

6 *The Works of Jeremy Bentham*, ed. by John Bowring (Edinburgh: W. Tait, 1843), Vol. III, pp. 248, 249.

7 An eighteenth-century writer, Daines Barrington, remarks that "The oldest conveyance we have any account of, viz. that of the cave of Mach-

pelah, from the sons of Heth to Abraham [Genesis xxxiii], hath many unnecessary and redundant words." *Observations on the Statutes* (London: W. Bowyer, 1766), p. 159.

8 Barrington suggests the very different theory that prolixity in "the modern statutes" has "in a great measure arisen from the use of printing," since "when manuscript copies are to be dispersed, the trouble of copying an unnecessary word is considered, but a page or two additional in print neither adds much to trouble or expense." *Ibid.*, pp. 158–159.

9 *Works*, p. 271a.

10 I owe the information contained in this paragraph to Frederick Pollock and Frederic William Maitland, *The History of English Law before the Time of Edward I*, 2nd ed. (2 vols.; Cambridge: Cambridge University Press, 1899), Vol. I, pp. 81–86.

11 Almost any current form-book will be found to afford illustrations. I have taken these examples from F. B. Tiffany, *Legal and Business Forms*, 2nd ed. rev. by William Cutler (St. Paul, Minn.: West, 1927), Form 5, p. 273, and Form 30, p. 1284.

12 These examples are quoted by Frederick Pollock in *A First Book of Jurisprudence*, 3rd ed. (London: Macmillan, 1911), p. 296, the first from "Rolle's *Reports* (i, 189)," the second from "Dyer's *Reports* (188b, notes added in 1688)." For further illustrations see *Les Reports des Cases en les Ans des Roys Edward V. Richard III. Henrie vij. & Henrie viij* (London, 1679), pp. 4, 5, and *passim*, and Jean Latch, *Plusieurs Tres-Bons Cases . . . es Trois Premiers Ans du Raign du Feu Roy Charles le Premier* (London, 1661), p. 120, and *passim*.

13 All of these expressions occur in documents now in my possession or custody, memorializing transactions to which I have been a party, whether in an individual or fiduciary capacity.

14 *Egyptian Literature*, introduction by Epiphanius Wilson (New York: Colonial Press, 1901), pp. 282–284.

15 *Ibid.*, p. 198.

16 According to E. M. Thompson in the *Encyclopaedia Britannica*, 13th ed., voc. "Seals," seals date from four and a half millennia B.C.; and their use as the guarantee of the authenticity of documents was known to Roman law and, after a lapse in the dark ages, was revived in the Merovingian and Carolingian chanceries and became general once more.

17 See G. W. and Lillie S. Botsford, eds., *A Source-Book of Ancient History* (New York: Macmillan, 1917), pp. 29–31 and 351–353.

18 *Die Gesetze der Anglesachsen. Erster Band: Text und Uebersetzung*, by F. Liebermann (Halle, a.S.: Max Niemeyer, 1903), pp. 1ff.

19 See Dorothy Bethurum's article, "Stylistic Features of the Old English Laws," *Modern Language Review*, Vol. XXVII (1932), pp. 263–279, especially pp. 264–269. As to the aesthetics of versified dooms, what is there to say except that, as the only verse form known to our forebears in the preliterate period, their heroic verse was the only convenient form of expression available for any content requiring day-to-day reference?

20 Botsford, *Source-Book*, pp. 450; trans. by R. R. Blews.

21 *Ancient Law* (1861) (New York: Dutton (Everyman's Library), 1931), p. 187.

22 *Ibid.*, pp. 91, 119–121, 192.

23 *Ibid.*, pp. 119, 121.

24 Harry Bresslau, *Handbuch der Urkundenlehre*, 2nd ed. (2 vols.; Leipzig: Veit, 1915), Vol. I, pp. 49, 50.

25 I owe the information contained in this and the two preceding paragraphs to Bresslau, *loc. cit.*

26 Joshua Williams, *Principles of the Law of Real Property*, 23rd ed., revised by T. Cyprian Williams (London: Sweet & Maxwell, 1920), p. 161.

27 *Ibid.*, p. 166.

28 *Ibid.*, pp. 165–166.

29 *Ancient Law*, pp. 123–124.

30 In the oldest codes, such as those referred to on p. 100, though these have sometimes been attributed to a mythical or semi-mythical lawgiver acting in a remote past (e.g., Jehovah or Solon), nothing in the form of any particular law reveals or suggests the lawgiver's identity. Each rule is stated as an independent, quite impersonal proposition, thus: "If a man practise brigandage and be captured, that man shall be put to death" (one of the laws of Hammurabi, in Botsford, *Source-Book*, p. 29); "Let there be no intermarriage between patricians and plebeians" (one of the laws of the Twelve Tables, in Botsford, p. 352); "If one cuts off another's index finger, let him pay nine shillings" (one of the dooms of Aethelbert of Kent, in Liebermann, *Die Gesetze der Anglesachsen*, p. 6).

31 The *Variae* of Cassiodorus (Theodor Mommsen, ed., *Monumenta Germaniae Historica, Auctores Antiquissimi* (Berlin: Weidmannos, 1894), Vol. 12), compiled from the archives of the court of Ravenna about 537, are said to represent ancient rather than medieval usage. See Bresslau, *Handbuch*, Vol. II, p. 241. The *Commentarii Magistratuum* of republican Rome and the *Legis Actiones* of about 450 B.C. may be actual examples of the republican formularies mentioned by Cicero (*De Legibus*, I, iv, 14, and elsewhere). On these, and related evidence, see Bresslau, *Handbuch*, Vol. II, pp. 227ff, and his notes.

32 See Eugène de Rozière, ed., *Liber Diurnus ou Recueil des Formules Usitées par la Chancellerie Pontificale du Ve au XIe Siècle* (Paris, 1869), and Bresslau, *Handbuch*, Vol. II, pp. 241–247. For bibliography and discussion of later formularies see Bresslau, Ch. XIII, and Arthur Giry, *Manuel de Diplomatique* (Paris: Hachette, 1894), Livre IV, Ch. i.

33 First published in *Works*, Vol. III, pp. 231–283.

34 Published in New York by Macmillan in 1928.

35 *Medieval Rhetoric and Poetic*, p. 215.

36 Ludwig Rockinger, *Briefsteller und Formelbücher des elften bis vierzehnten Jahrhunderts*, in *Quellen und Eröterungen zur Bayerischen und Deutschen Geschichte* (Munich: Georg Franz, 1863), Band IX.

37 *Ibid.*, p. 19.

38 *Ibid.*, p. 213.

39 *Ibid.*, p. 421.

40 Hermann Baerwald, ed., *Das Baumgartenberger Formelbuch*, in *Fontes Austriacarum*, 2te Abtheilung, *Diplomataria et Acta*, Band xxv (Vienna: Aus der Kaiserlich-Königlichen Hof- und Staatsdruckerei, 1866), pp. 1–2. The text concerning the etymology runs in Latin: "causa autem inventionis huius [*scil.* dictaminis] fuit duplex: prima ut per dictamen seu per epistolam amicorum secreta celarentur, unde dicitur 'epistola' ab 'epistolon' grece, quod latine dicitur 'abscondo' . . ." The now received etymology of "epistola," which makes it simply something sent, typically a message (Greek ἐπιστολή

being a substantival equivalent of ἐπιστέλλω was presumably unknown to the writer of the *Formularius*. He apparently finds the idea of concealment in the element "-stola" taken in the sense it bears when uncompounded, namely that of a robe (English "stole"), therefore a garment beneath which the wearer can hide his identity. Curiously enough the Greek cognate of "stola," στολή, is also related to στέλλω and its compounds; but I take the significant point about our author's etymology to be not the accidental plausibility of it but its apparent betrayal of the influence of a perverse rhetorical principle of wide currency from ancient times well into the Renaissance, namely that concealment of meaning is a prime virtue in any piece of writing.

41   A. F. Conard, "New Ways to Write Laws," *Yale Law Journal*, Vol. LVI (1947), pp. 458ff, quoted by Read and MacDonald, *Cases*, pp. 914–935. The present reference is to the latter work, pp. 914 and 918–920.

42   D. L. Kennedy, *Drafting Bills for the Minnesota Legislature* (St. Paul, Minn.: West, 1946), p. 7, quoted in Read and MacDonald, *Cases*, p. 914.

43   A. F. Conard; see Read and MacDonald, *Cases*, p. 915.

44   *Ibid.*, p. 923.

45   *Ibid.*, p. 927.

46   *Ibid.*, pp. 928, 929.

47   *Ibid.*, p. 924.

48   *Drafting Rules and Suggestions Prepared by the Committee on Legislative Drafting of the National Conference of Commissioners on Uniform State Laws in Accordance with Resolutions Adopted by the Conference at Saratoga in 1917, and Amended by the Conference at Cleveland in 1918, and Further Amended by the Conference at Washington in 1932*, quoted by Read and MacDonald, *Cases*, p. 936.

49   A. F. Conard; see Read and MacDonald, *Cases*, p. 932.

50   Anticipated by Jeremy Bentham (*Works*, Vol. III, p. 260), the modern rule is to use a single word or short phrase in place of many a cumbersome phrase formerly current in the jargon, as for example: "adjudged" for "ordered, adjudged, and decreed"; "conclusive" for "final and conclusive"; "evidences of indebtedness" for "bonds, notes, checks, drafts, and other evidences of indebtedness"; "shall" for "is hereby authorized and it shall be his duty." I have taken these examples from a long list given by W. B. Henderson, *Report of Revisor of Statutes to the Minnesota Legislature* (1941), p. 60, as quoted in Read and MacDonald, *Cases*, p. 938.

51   *Works*, Vol. III, p. 237.

52   See Fred Rodell, *Woe Unto You, Lawyers!* (New York: Reynal & Hitchcock, 1939), pp. 7ff, 18lf, 192, 193, 270, and more or less *passim*. He argues that such terms as "felony," "misdemeanor," "tort," and "consideration," instead of simply designating facts, color facts with "abstract general principles," and that "none of these principles has any real or necessary relation to the solid substance of human affairs." He would still have constitutions and statutes "all written in ordinary English" — but how without **principles**? Or if with them, to what purpose, if, as he assures us, "principles are intrinsically meaningless" and likewise "silly"? "The Highest Law of the Land," in his view, is nothing better than a "vast structure of abracadabra." Jerome Frank remarks of the word "law" that it "drips with ambiguity" (*Law and the Modern Mind* (New York: Brentanos, 1930; Coward-McCann, 1949), preface to the sixth printing, 1949, p. vi). See also Thurman Arnold on "estoppel," "trust," "law," "equity," and "justice" (*The Symbols of Government* (New

Haven, Conn.: Yale University Press, 1935), pp. 28, 44f, 62, 63), and Stuart Chase on these other "weasel words in the jargon of lawyers": "manifest intention," "prudent," "negligence," "freedom of contract," "good faith" (*The Tyranny of Words*, p. 324).

53 *Works*, Vol. III, p. 270.

54 See note 52 above.

55 See note 52 above.

56 Chase, *The Tyranny of Words*, p. 324.

57 *The Symbols of Government*, pp. 39–42.

58 As by Chaucer. See pp. 117–118.

59 E. M. W. Tillyard, *Shakespeare's History Plays* (New York: Macmillan, 1947), p. 24.

60 Published by the Princeton University Press, Princeton, N.J., in 1940.

61 *The Canterbury Tales*, A–322, E–16–18, and A–638–646, respectively.

62 *The Chronicles of Froissart*, trans. by John Bourchier, Lord Berners, ed. by G. C. Macaulay (London: Macmillan, 1904), p. 382.

63 Garrett Mattingly, *The Armada* (Boston: Houghton Mifflin, 1959), p. 215, here quoted with the kind permission of the Houghton Mifflin Company.

64 Edward Gibbon, *The History of the Decline and Fall of the Roman Empire*, 2nd ed. (6 vols.; London: W. Strahan, 1776–88), Vol. VI, Ch. LXX, p. 605, and Vol. V, Ch. XLIX, p. 155, respectively.

65 John Galt, *Annals of the Parish*, ed. by G. Baillie Macdonald (New York: Dutton (Everyman's Library), 1926), p. 23.

66 *Ibid.*, p. 22.

67 *Ibid.*, pp. 1, 4.

Index

INDEX

INDEX

Coleridge, Samuel Taylor: concludes *The Rime of the Ancient Mariner* with summary, 33; mentioned, 85

Commentaries (Caesar), 106

Commissioners on Uniform State Laws, 113

Commonplaces: Burke's use of, 26; in prophetic discourse, 70

Conciseness: in prophetic discourse, 71, 74, 78, 81

Conclusio (rhetorical term), 109

Cōpie (or copiousness): proper and improper use of, 10, 19, 27; in legal instruments, 94

Corineus, 116

Correlatives: in deliberative prose, 20

Coupé: variety of the prophetic style, 71, 74, 78, 81

Cowley, Abraham, 84

Critics, literary, 10–11

Croll, Morris W.: co-editor of Lyly's *Euphues*, 11; on the Stoic stylists, 73–79 *passim*; mentioned, 83

Cromwell, Oliver, 12, 84

Cursus (rhetorical term), 108

Cuthbert, Saint: Aelfric's sermon on, 59–60

Daniel, Samuel, 83, 84

Darwin, Charles, 42, 43, 45

David, King of Judah and Israel, 98

De Constantia (Lipse), 83

Declaration of Independence, 97

Decline and Fall of the Roman Empire, The (Gibbon), 31, 121

Décousu style: variety of prophetic style, 78–81 *passim*

Defense of Poesie (Sidney): Ciceronian influence in, 45

Deliberative argument: looks to the future, 23–25; premisses in, 23–25; practical efficacy of, 24

Deliberative style, 6, 8–10, 12, 13, 16, second chapter *passim*

Democracy, 22

Demosthenes: First Olynthiac of described, 33–34; quoted, 34–36; mentioned, 9

"Deor" (Anglo-Saxon poem), 56

Descartes, René, 45

DeVoto, Bernard: tumbling style of

in *We Accept with Pleasure*, 64; quoted, 64–65; mentioned, 67, 69

Dialogue Concerning Heresies and Matters of Religion, A (More), 61–62

Dialogues of Plato: style of, 73

Diana of the Crossways (Meredith): quoted, 87

Dickens, Charles: title *Great Expectations* cited, 31; indenture style of in *Pickwick Papers*

Diction: of tumbling discourse, 16, 57–58, 62, 68; of deliberative discourse, 21–22; of expository discourse, 40; of prophetic discourse, 74–75, 78, 86; of legal instruments, 96–98. *See also* Metaphor

Dido, 122

Diogenes Laertius, 74

Diogenes the Babylonian (Stoic philosopher of undetermined date B.C.): cited by Diogenes Laertius on Stoic rhetoric, 74

Diplomatic (the science), 91, 107

Dispositive document, 102

Dobrée, Bonamy, 5

Documents: use of in Roman law, 13, 100–103

Donatus, Aelius (grammarian of fourth century A.D.), 5

Dooms, the, of Aethelbert of Kent (ca. *600* A.D.), 100

Drafting, legal: general expressions distrusted in, 94; modern authorities on, 110–115 *passim*; sixth chapter *passim*

"Dream of the Rood, The" (Anglo-Saxon poem), 67

Dryden, John, 76

Edgeworth, Maria: indenture style of in *Castle Rackrent*, 123

Eliot, George (Mary Ann Evans): an episode of *Middlemarch* described, 34; quoted, 37–38; mentioned, 67, 69

Eliot, Sir John (*1592–1632*), 12, 84

Eloquence: philosophers' and scientists' distrust of, 22–23; of Nestor, 24; didactic form of different from deliberative, 42

Emerson, Ralph Waldo, 80, 86

Epic poetry: influence on historiography and prose fiction, 32
Epictetus: style of illustrated, 75–76; mentioned, 83
Epistle, see Letter
Epistola (rhetorical term), 103, 108
Equation, the typical expository statement, 39
Erasmus, Desiderius: satirist of Ciceronian pedantry, 28–29
Esau, 31
Essay, 72, fourth chapter passim
Essays (Bacon), 13, 77–78
Euclid, 8, 45
Euphues (Lyly), 50–52
Euphuism: essentially a scientific-didactic style, 7–8, 11, 45–49; found in epideictic oratory and philosophical discourse and called the "genus medium" or "genus floridum" by Cicero and Quintilian, 46–49; air of authority of, 49; style of in Euphues described, 50–51
Exclamation: use of in deliberative oratory, 21
Exordium (rhetorical term), 109
Expanded lines: in Anglo-Saxon poems, 63
Expository style: 7, 8, 9, 11, 12–13, 14, 15, 16, 20, 27, 33, third chapter passim
Ezekiel, 83

Fiction, prose: antecedents of, 31–32; kinship with deliberative and forensic argument, 32–38
Fielding, Henry: title The History of Tom Jones, a Foundling cited, 31
Fifteenth Century Translation as an Influence on English Prose (Workman), 117
Finnegans Wake (Joyce), 88
"Finnsburg Fragment," the (Anglo-Saxon poem), 66
Flesch, Rudolf, 23
Fletcher, John, 119
Forensic oratory, 6, 12, 26–27
Form: meaning of in critical parlance, 4
Formularius de Modo Prosandi (anonymous fourteenth-century rhetoric): quoted,109–110

Foundacion of Rhetorike, The (Rainolde), 28
Frank, Jerome, 112
Frankish law: nomenclature in, 103
French: terms from in English law, 96; use of by English court reporters, 97
Friar Daw Topias (interlocutor of Jack Upland), 61
Froissart, Jean: style of Chronicles of as translated by Lord Berners, 118–119; quoted, 119
Fuller, Thomas, 84

Galen(us), Claudius, 8
Galt, John: indenture style of in Annals of the Parish, 123; quoted, 124
Garden of Cyrus, The (Browne): quoted, 78
George, Saint, 122
Germanic poetry: style of, 13. See also Alliterative-accentual verse
Gestures: in deliberative oratory, 21
Gettysburg Address: style of examined, 52; quoted, 52–53
Gibbon, Edward: title The Decline and Fall of the Roman Empire cited, 31; use of indenture style, 121; mentioned, 32
Gogmagog, 116
Gorgias (orator of fifth century B.C.), 7
Gray, Thomas, 10
Great Expectations (Dickens), 31
Ground leases: language of, 98
Gulliver's Travels (Swift): quoted, 67–68

Hammurabi, Laws of (twentieth century B.C.), 100
Hardy, Thomas, 32
Harley Street doctors' bills: objective style of, 106
Harris, Joel Chandler: quoted, 68, 90
Harvey, Gabriel: style of, 60; quarrel with Nashe, 69
Harvey, Richard, 62
Hazlitt, William, 84–85
Hendrickson, G. L., 74
Henry Esmond (Thackeray), 123
Hermogenes (Alexandrian rhetorician of second century A.D.), 8

INDEX

Hero and Leander: Nashe's version of story of quoted, 62–63
Herodotus, 32, 33
Hildesheim, Ludolf of, 108
Historians: of literature, 11–12; Greek, 32, 33–34, 116; mentioned, 44
Historiography: antecedents of, 14, 31–32; kinship with deliberative and forensic argument, 32–37; change in concept of, 119. *See also* Fiction
History of King Richard the Third, The (More), 119
History of the Peloponnesian War (Thucydides): quoted, 36–37; mentioned, 31–34 *passim*
History of the Rebellion (Clarendon), 119
History of the World (Raleigh), 119
Homer, 24, 31
Hooker, Richard: Ciceronian influence on, 45
Hosmer, Henry B.: quoted, 114
Hyde, Edward, Earl of Clarendon, 119
Hyde Park, 49
Hymns, 116

Iliad, 31
Incremental effects: usually unimportant in exposition, 41
Indenture style: influence of in nonlegal literature, 116–124; sixth chapter *passim*
Instrument, legal, *see* Legal instrument
Interpretation of law, 27
Isaac, 31
Isocrates, 9
Isolde, 122
Ivanhoe (Scott), 120

Jack Upland, 61
Jack Wilton, 122
Jacob, 31
Jeremiah, 83
Jezebel, 100
Joab, 98
John Buncle, 84
John Maundevile, Sir, 117
Joyce, James: *Finnegans Wake* of quoted, 88

Judges, 110, 111. *See also* Lawyers

Kant, Immanuel, 45
Kennings, 57–58
Krapp, George Philip: quoted, 60–61

Laban, 31
Lamb, Charles: quoted, 82; mentioned, 11, 79, 80, 84
Landbooks: use of Latin in in England, 96
Langland, William: humor of, 58; quoted, 58–59; influence of, 60, 61; made fictitious character (Piers the Plowman) vehicle of his message, 61
Latin: terms from in English law, 96
Launcelot, Sir, 122
Law: ancient Roman, 13, 100–103; French and Latin terms in English courts and documents of, 96, 97; Babylonian, 100; Lombardic, 103. *See also* Dooms
Lawyers: rise of profession in late Middle Ages, 101, 115; satirized, 117–118, 119; modern, on drafting, 110, 111; conservative as to language, 114; mentioned, 9, 90, 97. *See also* Drafting, legal
Lay (form of narrative poem), 55
Leander, 62–63
Legal instrument: forms and style of, sixth chapter *passim. See also* Drafting, legal; Letter
Lenten Stuffe (Nashe): quoted, 62–63
Letter (i.e., epistle): archetype of the modern legal instrument, 13, 103–104; earliest uses of, 98–100, 105; as a literary form, 104
Lewis, Wyndham: quoted, 88
Liber Diurnus (anonymous rhetoric, ca. 800 A.D.), 107
Life and Opinions of John Buncle, The (Amory), 84
Lincoln, Abraham: style of the Gettysburg Address of examined, 52; the Address quoted, 52–53
Lipse, Juste, 83, 84
Livery of seisin, 105
Livy (Livius), Titus, 117
Logbooks: style of, 49
Logic, Aristotelian, 83

[145]

INDEX

Olynthus, 34
On Conciliation with America (Burke), 24–26
Organon (Aristotle): quoted, 40–41
Origin of Species, The (Darwin), 42, 43, 45
Osorius (Jeronymo Osorio, *1506–1580*), 28

Palestine, 98
Pamela Andrews, 122
Pappe with a Hatchet (Lyly), 62
Paradoxes: in prophetic discourse, 70
Paratactic style: of Bible, 116–117
Parenthesis: in deliberative oratory, 20, 21
Particulars: enumeration of in legal instruments, 94
Past and Present (Carlyle): quoted, 85
Paul, Saint: Stoic thought in, 73; mentioned, 83
Pericles, 8, 9; Athens under rule of, 22
Petitio (rhetorical term), 109
Pharaoh, the: diplomatic letters to, 98–100; mentioned, 98
Pickwick Papers (Dickens), 120
Piers Plowman, 58–59, 60, 61
"Plants: Cytology" (H. W. T. Wager): quoted, 41
Platonic dialogues: style of, 73
Pliny the Elder, 45
Plotinus, 8
Poetry: Germanic, 13; history "borders too closely on" (so Antonius according to Cicero), 14; epic, 32; images associated with, in euphuistic prose, 51; idea generally assumed to be inseparable from the word in, 55; Anglo-Saxon, 56, 63; of idea and diction in legal instruments, 97–98. *See also* Alliterative-accentual verse
Pollock, Frederick, 96
Pope, Alexander, 76
Premisses: in deliberative argument, 23–25
Principles of Geology (Lyell), 42
Prolixity: in legal instruments, 94–95
Prophetic Books of the Bible, 72
Prophetic style, fourth chapter *passim*

Prose: a negative category, 4; etymology of the word, 4–5; theory of narrative styles of, 14–15; idea generally assumed to be separable from the word in, 55. *See also* Fiction, prose
Proverbs, The (of Solomon), 71
Ptolemy (Ptolemaeus), Claudius, 8
Punctuation: in legal instruments, 92–94, 111
Puritan philosophy, 84
Pym, John (*1584–1643*), 12, 84

Quackery, stylistic, 43–45
Quintilian(us), Marcus Fabius: uses term "prosa oratio," 5; influence of, 6; on historiography, 14; kind of rhetoric taught by, 18; on variety of form in successive units of discourse, 20; on ancient euphuism, 46; on the style of Seneca, 76

Rabelais, François: characterized by Paul Stapfer, 68; satirical of lawyers, 119; quoted, 65
Rainolde, Richard, 28
Raleigh, Sir Walter (*1552?–1618*), 119
Raphael Hythloday, 62
Rationes Dictandi (Alberic of Monte Cassino, eleventh century), 108
Read, Sir Herbert, 5
Read, Horace E.: co-author of *Cases and Other Materials on Legislation*, 110, 111
Rebekah, 31
Reference: forward and backward in deliberative discourse, 19
Renaissance: traditional definition of, 44
Republican Rome, 22
Rhetoric: ancient classical, 6, 10, 18–20; ancient postclassical, 6–7; influence of classical, 6–7, 8, 18, 29–30, 32, 107–108; Second Sophistic school of at Alexandria, 6–7, 8–9; disparaged, 8, 22–23; limitations of manuals of, 8–10; Stoic, 74
Rhetoric (Aristotle), 6
Rhetorica ad Herennium, 7
Rhetorical question: use of in deliberative discourse, 20, 21

INDEX